Look for His miracles Eph...

HOME RUNS
FOR HEAVEN

Great is God's Faithfulness!

Gary

LAM 3:21-25

HOME RUNS *for* HEAVEN

A Story of God's Faithfulness
Told in Two Voices

PASTOR GARY MCCUSKER AND
CINDY KAY ZIMMERMANN

XULON PRESS ELITE

Xulon Press Elite
2301 Lucien Way #415
Maitland, FL 32751
407.339.4217
www.xulonpress.com

Front Cover Idea Tiffany Funk

Front Cover Baseball Photo Lori A. Brundage

Back Cover Photo Patrick and Pastor Gary McCusker at PEPC. Photo Credit Cindy Kay Zimmermann

Printed in the United States of America.

ISBN-13: 978-1-54566-442-1

Dedication

This book is dedicated to the memory of Patrick Chandler Zimmermann. May the lessons he taught us help us walk ever more closely with our Lord and Savior, Jesus Christ.

Acknowledgments

We would like to thank Debi McCusker, Steve Zimmermann, and our families for their love, many personal sacrifices, and unwavering support throughout the years. The Barila and Cahill families gently told us about God's love for us. In addition, we extend sincere gratitude to the Zimmermann's home fellowship group and our church family at Parker Evangelical Presbyterian Church for truly being the hands and feet of Jesus. Next, we thank the many special people who supported and encouraged Patrick in his final years of life. A special thank you goes to Tiffany Funk, for creating Patrick's memorial video and inspiring our book's cover. We are incredibly grateful for the words of encouragement from the friends and family members who urged us to share Patrick's story with the world. Julia Williams, Kimberly and John Neininger, Lydia and Harry Lightner, Randy McFarland, Linette Miller, Joe Bradley, Bill Watkins, Farland Bottoms, and Pastor Doug Resler provided prayer, input, and guidance at just the right moments in our journey and emboldened us along the way to publication. Finally, we extend a special thank you to our team at Xulon Publishing, for bringing *Home Runs for Heaven* to completion.

Contents

- What Day Is It?
- God's Plan, Not Mine
- Pepperoni Kisses
- Yearning for Perfect Peace

- To Board or Not to Board, That Is
  the Question
- Angels Watching Over Me
- Noisy Silence
- Is There Turndown Service in Heaven?
- Is the Angel Here Because I'm Dying?
- Longing to Be in Heaven
- Watch the Animals
- A Cowboy's Last Trail Ride?
- Lord, I Am Weary
- Crash Course in Christianity
- Rearranging Furniture
- Higher Ground
- Wildflowers Everywhere
- Count It All Joy
- God's Sense of Humor
- Caregiving 101

- Sophomore Achievement Award—A Gentle
  Soul with a Big Heart
- Ode on a Strawberry Rhubarb Pie
- Of Mosquitoes, Music, and Memories
- A Single Tear
- Don't Forget the Guy in the Wheelchair
- God's Love Personified
- Joy Comes in the Morning
- A Bad Day Fishin'
- The Angel's Back

Contents

Preface

Dear Reader,

You are about to dive into a story of God's faithfulness that will take you across two continents. You'll hear the perspectives of Reverend Gary McCusker, Pastor of Care Ministries at Parker Evangelical Presbyterian Church and Cindy Kay Zimmermann throughout the story. We have printed Pastor Gary's words on a gray background to make it easier to understand when we change voices.

As we read through the manuscript in preparation for publication, Randy McFarland, a dear brother in Christ, suggested we write a preface to share with readers why we wrote this book.

In my role as a pastor, called by God to be His ambassador of the love and grace of the Gospel, I am more than eager to share the compassion of Jesus Christ with anyone who enters my sphere of ministry. On a Sunday afternoon in March of 2015, I responded to a telephone call received at the church office. I drove to my favorite coffee shop to meet a mother and her son who had questions about heaven. My normal prayer on the way to these kinds of situations is, "Lord, prepare me to be your agent of love, truth, and grace.

May you be glorified in all I think, do, or say." Little did I realize that my conversation with Cindy and her son, Patrick, would begin an incredible transformation for him, for his parents, for our church, and for myself. It was a privilege to observe the Holy Spirit capture Patrick's heart and life with a love for Jesus and for him to believe the glorious promise of a future home in heaven. My association with Patrick changed forever how I communicate the message about our eternal home with Jesus Christ our Redeemer and with God our heavenly Father.

It is my hope and prayer that the story of Patrick's joy on a very difficult journey will inspire you to live nearer our Father's heart and that it will teach you how you may be more effective in serving as a conduit of His love to and for others.

I prayed for God to guide my hands while I typed the answer to Randy's question about why we wrote this book. What started out as CaringBridge journal entries quickly morphed from medical updates about my son, Patrick, to a description of my family's journey of faith. I started adding Bible verses and Christian songs that were meaningful to me. Yes, it's personal. Yes, the emotions are raw. There were times when I would be sobbing so hard that I couldn't see the computer screen while I was typing. It was as if God were speaking through my pain and into my heart. After reading my CaringBridge entries, several friends suggested we share Patrick's story with others.

There are times when I still wrestle with God. To be honest, I don't like the plan he has for our lives, but I am slowly learning to accept it. I don't understand why I couldn't have a "normal" childhood followed by a "typical" marriage with lots of kids and grand-kids. Those things haven't been in God's plan for me. Lydia Lightner, a sweet sister in Christ, recently asked me a pointed question, "Where would you be in your walk with the Lord if you had been given the life *you* wanted?" This book describes the odyssey that God sent us on—not at all what I had planned.

So, if you find yourself walking a journey that you would not have chosen, or walking beside someone who is, please look for examples of God's faithfulness, tiny miracles really, that show you that you are not by yourself on your journey. We hope and pray that reading this book helps you know that you are not alone in your pain and that God is right there beside you, waiting for you to lean on Him.

Foreword

I remember first meeting Patrick Zimmermann. It was in a local coffee shop where I spent a lot of time. He had just finished a conversation with his mom and Pastor Gary McCusker, and it was clear something special had taken place. Everyone was still drying the tears in their eyes as they told me about Patrick's decision to follow Christ. From that moment forward, God not only did a mighty work in the Zimmermann family, but in the family at Parker Evangelical Presbyterian Church (PEPC). I often tell our congregation that our church changes every time God brings us a new family to love. That certainly has been the case with the Zimmermanns. Patrick taught us all about the sufficiency of God's grace, as he fought for his life. He always had a joy about him, a playfulness that would catch you by surprise, and a peace that passed all understanding. Patrick trusted Jesus with all his heart, and though his physical body was wasting away, his inner nature was being renewed each day by God's Spirit.

One could not help but be impacted by Patrick's contagious faith. Certainly, his mother and father will testify to this, and you will read much of their story in the pages that follow. I cannot begin to tell you the impact Patrick has made on our church family. His faithful witness continues to serve as an inspiration. His story is one that is told over and over again. His memory is kept alive by those who had the privilege of walking the journey with him, from this world to the next. We remember, especially, his baptism and his joy, at seeing his father give his life to Christ and his parents reaffirm their baptisms as well. We remember him handing out bulletins at the door, as he found ways to serve, even through his disability. Perhaps, most of all, we remember his smile and two thumbs up.

Second Corinthians 1:3–4 (ESV) says, "Blessed be the God and Father of our Lord Jesus Christ, the Father of mercies and God of all comfort, who comforts us in all our affliction, so that we may be able to comfort those who are in any affliction, with the comfort with which we ourselves are comforted by God." Steve and Cindy have walked through the valley of the shadow of death. They have tasted the fear and plumbed the depths of grief. They suffered tremendously, but they never walked alone. Jesus was with them every step of the way and so was their church family. It was one of the greatest privileges of my life to be part of this journey with them and to watch them emerge from the darkness, into the light. They are living examples of what the apostle Paul wrote so many thousands of years ago. They comfort others with great tenderness. They come alongside others and offer encouragement. They pray fervently. They minister faithfully. They listen patiently. Having experienced the comfort that comes only from Christ, they now share that comfort with others.

Foreword

I hope and pray that you—the reader—will find comfort in their story, inspiration in their witness, and strength from their journey as you make your way through whatever challenges you face. May God bless you as you read and ponder the words of this book.

—Rev. Dr. Doug Resler
Parker Evangelical Presbyterian Church

Chapter One

A Divine Appointment

"Why am I on this plane, Lord? Please guide my hands and feet, because I'm not sure why I'm doing this," I whispered as I stared out of the tiny window on the American Airlines flight from Miami, Florida, to Port au Prince, Haiti. Playful, dragon-shaped clouds danced above aqua ribbons wrapping the Bahamas' tiny islets that dotted the navy-blue Atlantic Ocean. Words from the song "Oceans" washed through my mind. Here I was, just a baby Christian, with a long history of trust issues, stepping out in a huge leap of faith, following a God I was only beginning to know.

In June of 2017, the Lord had called thirty-seven of us from Parker Evangelical Presbyterian Church (PEPC) on a mission trip to serve at an orphanage in Fond Blanc, Haiti, 2,400 miles away from our comfortable homes in Parker, Colorado. This trip was taking me, a nearly sixty-year-old woman who likes the temperature to remain constant at seventy-two degrees, *way* out of my comfort zone. We were headed to an impoverished country where June's average afternoon high temperature, on any given day, was ninety-five degrees.

God called. I answered. Here I was, with 708 miles of flying time to reflect on the events that led me to embark on this adventure in faith. I thought back to the time I met Pastor Gary at Fika Coffee House. On March 22, 2015, I sat nervously sipping water from a clear plastic bottle while my fifteen-year-old son, Patrick, nibbled his lemon pastry at a round table in the middle of a bustling coffee shop. We were hoping for answers from a pastor. I eyed the door, waiting.

Patrick, devastated by the death of Hope, one of our horse rescues, had questions about heaven that I couldn't answer. Earlier that week, I had called a friend's church, PEPC, hoping someone there could help us ease Patrick's pain. I didn't know that our lives were about to change forever. Soon an athletic-looking, fifty-something man with kind, hazel eyes would step into Fika and join us at our table, beginning a conversation that would set into motion a series of events that we could not begin to fathom. Like an invisible pebble dropping into a pond and sending out silent ripples, that conversation would change our lives, and the lives of countless others. Blessedly, on that sunny spring afternoon, we also didn't know that just five hundred and fifty days later, we would all be together in a much different setting. But God knew.

Chapter Two

Patrick's NPC Journey

A Horse Called Hope

> "And we know that in all things God works for the good of those who love him, who have been called according to his purpose" (Rom 8:28).

One of the many ways that God showed His love to us, was through the kind people He sent into our lives at just the right time. Our family was involved in a horse rescue called Drifter's Hearts of Hope (DHOH). Serving with other special needs students gave Patrick and us a much-needed sense of community. Those students and their families became an integral part of our lives. Our first three rescues from the kill pen were given new names—Hope, Spirit, and Clarity. We weren't planning to adopt a horse with health challenges like Hope, but she was literally being attacked by another horse in the pen, and that is why she went home to DHOH. The kids worked together to love and care for the horses, raise funds for their upkeep, and find them homes. Patrick did not understand why any of our rescue horses would die. Hope was an older horse with Cushing's disease. She enjoyed lots of love and care from the children before she developed serious complications. She had a gentle death. Two other horses stood watch. I was one of those who were holding her as she passed.

Our chat with Pastor Gary became a conversation about faith in Jesus. Pastor Gary led Patrick to Christ right there in the middle of that busy coffee house. The three of us cried tears of joy together. It seemed fitting to me that God, the author of the universe, chose a horse called Hope to lead Patrick to Him.

We then discussed the possibility of having Patrick baptized the following weekend, on Palm Sunday, at PEPC. I was concerned that Patrick would have a seizure during his baptism. Patrick was experiencing difficulties with slurred speech and had recently started having seizures. We didn't know what was causing the gradual changes, and we were working with doctors at Children's Hospital to figure it out. Patrick had received earlier diagnoses of attention deficit disorder (ADD) and later, autism. We were waiting on genetic testing results. We talked about how to keep him safe during such an emotional event as baptism. A part of me was afraid to go home after our meeting with Pastor Gary, because I would have to tell my husband, Steve, the news. Our marriage was not strong. He wouldn't share in our joy. Quite the opposite. He would, in fact, be enraged and suspicious. I feared his reaction, for he was an unbeliever.

Patrick's Baptism—The Next Step on the Journey Home

> He gives strength to the weary, and to him who lacks might He increases power. Though youths grow weary and tired, and vigorous young men stumble badly, yet those who wait for the LORD will gain new strength. They will mount up with wings like eagles. They will run and not get tired. They will walk and not become weary. (Is 40:29–31 NASB)

As I had feared, Steve was infuriated when I shared the news of Patrick's decision to accept Christ. He also expressed concern that Patrick would be publicly humiliated in some way. Pastor Gary assured us that he would be sensitive to Patrick's needs. Steve was suspicious when we visited the church in preparation for Patrick's baptism. He wondered if the people meeting there were going to try to *sell* Christianity to us (They didn't). I privately implored Steve to allow Patrick to have his faith without questioning it. Thankfully, he respected my request to keep his own lack of faith to himself. He didn't grill Patrick on his decision. I knew friends were praying for Steve's heart to soften and for him to accept Jesus Christ as his Lord and Savior. What I didn't know was that they were also praying for me to develop a closer relationship with the Lord.

The next weekend, Patrick took the first step on his long road home. He chose to be baptized on Palm Sunday, so he could walk with God. He stood with our dear friend, John Neininger. (He, along with his wife,

Kimberly, were the ones who had invited us to their church for so many years.) Patrick and John were joined by Max Cahill, Patrick's childhood friend who had modeled his own faith for Patrick when they were young. John read Patrick's verse from Isaiah 40 for him, since he was a little unsteady on his feet, he was especially emotional, and his speech was, at times, difficult to understand. Patrick's blue eyes filled with tears as Pastor Gary gently sprinkled water on his sandy blonde hair, baptizing him in the name of the Father, the Son, and the Holy Ghost.

Steve and I sat with friends in the front pews of what was to become our new church home. Some of Patrick's teachers and friends attended PEPC, and they welcomed us enthusiastically. It was all completely different from the worship we had experienced for so many years. I found myself searching for a hymnal. There weren't any. The song lyrics were on large screens. Things had changed *so much* in worship from when I had last attended a traditional church. There was a worship band with guitars and a drum set. Patrick, a total people person and music lover, enjoyed the service and wanted to go *every* Sunday! We began to attend PEPC each week. To my amazement, Steve, impressed by the thoughtful sermons he was hearing, wanted to attend faithfully *with* us! I understand now that God was already at work, answering my prayers, softening our hearts, creating a church family support system, and preparing us for the heartrending challenges just ahead on our journey.

Softly and Tenderly, Jesus was Calling to Us

God's handiwork has been compared to a tapestry.[1] I like to sew, and that metaphor speaks to me. We, here on Earth, can only see His artistry's messy back side, not the beautiful finished design that He is creating with each loving stitch. One of the first threads in God's plan was when He used Hope's death to connect us with Pastor Gary at PEPC. Patrick's grief was so great when Hope died that I needed to ask for help. God had carefully woven the circumstances for my phone call, through the actions of caring friends who had gently and consistently invited us to visit PEPC for events such as Missions Weekends and bell choir concerts. Having experienced that church's warm, welcoming atmosphere, I was comfortable calling PEPC when we had a faith crisis.

Steve grew up in a Presbyterian family and attended a Quaker school. He came to Christ as a teenager, but like me, his faith hadn't developed deep roots. His intellectual mind pitted his faith against his scientific college education. At that time, he didn't have a strong faith support system, and he didn't seek answers from a mentor in his church. He fell away from his faith, becoming an agnostic with a sharply critical and dismissive attitude toward people of faith.

Although the events at the coffee shop caught me by surprise, I didn't question Patrick's decision to accept Christ that day. Patrick and I had been attending Quaker meetings since he was an infant. Our choice of a church was a much-discussed compromise. I had been raised in the Lutheran faith, but when we were married by a judge at an outdoor ceremony, Steve and

I were about as far from our faith as we could be. I had not spent my life following Jesus—far from it. I had accepted Christ at a Billy Graham revival when I was thirteen years old. I had not built strong connections in my church family, and I walked away from my faith in my late teens. I thought of myself as a spiritual person, but I did not have a meaningful relationship with Jesus. I had wandered for forty years in a wilderness of my own making. I saw my youthful acceptance of Christ as a kind of "get out of hell free" card. I'm now embarrassed to admit that I saw myself as *beyond* needing the Lord, having developed a condescending attitude toward Christians, thinking my own faith was far more *evolved* than theirs.

Patrick's birth prompted me to seek a church home. I sat alone on Sundays in silent Quaker worship for fifteen years, while Patrick attended Quaker First Day School (Sunday school) and learned about faith in general terms. All the while, I was praying that God would show me how to be a better wife and that one day, Steve would sit in worship with me. Thankfully, Patrick had heard about Jesus from family members and friends who I believe God placed in our lives for just that purpose.

I have pondered God's incredible faithfulness to me throughout my life. Music is a huge part of who I am and how I think, so words from an old hymn I sang in church as a child help me look carefully at the events in my life and see how Jesus was softly and tenderly calling Steve and me back to Him as He wove the events of our lives together. I know now that He wanted us to be walking closely with Him as we entered the darkest valley of our lives.

A Little Child Shall Lead Them

"A little child shall lead them" (Is 11:6).

Forty-four days after Patrick was baptized, we got a phone call from our team at Children's Hospital. It's never good news when a neurologist calls you at home—at night. We received the results of our genetic testing. Steve and I had done our research about the possible results and what they meant for our future. We were sobbing when we shared the news with Patrick. He looked into our tear-stained blue eyes and said, "We shouldn't be crying. We should be laughing—because I'm going to heaven." He was so wise, even then.

Soon after that phone call, Pastor Gary accompanied us to the doctor's appointment where we were to receive Patrick's official diagnosis. He opened our meeting in prayer. The tiny exam room was crowded with several adults and Patrick's newly acquired wheelchair. After years of trying to find reasons for the changes we were seeing in Patrick, the testing showed that Patrick had an extremely rare genetic condition he had inherited from both of us. It was called Niemann-Pick Type C disease (NPC). NPC has been called Childhood Alzheimer's, because some of the symptoms *can* mimic Alzheimer's disease. In Patrick's case, some of his symptoms were indeed quite like Alzheimer's. He had developed rigid thinking and sometimes had violent episodes. This cruel disease had been inside Patrick's body since conception, slowly stealing his ability to think, walk, and speak. Pastor Gary maneuvered Patrick out of the small room and down to the hospital cafeteria.

The doctors told us about stage one trial medications and their side effects. *There were no guarantees.* They said the drugs could help improve Patrick's symptoms, could make them worse, or *they could do nothing.* We also learned that the trial medicine might cause deafness. One medicine was given through the spine. It would mean frequent airplane travel to where the medication was administered. Travel and changes in Patrick's schedule were hard on him. He was already showing autistic-like behaviors that made being in public difficult. Another trial medication was administered orally and would require significant changes in Patrick's diet, or it could cause serious gastrointestinal side effects. Patrick *loved* to eat. If he took the medicine, he would *not* be able to eat many of the foods he loved. We had a lot to think about and pray about. Pastor Gary returned with Patrick and closed our appointment with prayer. We went home to begin our "new normal."

Throughout our NPC journey, we promised Patrick we would be honest with him. If we knew something, we would share it with him. Patrick already *hated* the medicines we had to give him three times a day to prevent seizures. We told him about our treatment choices and what they would mean. Patrick emphatically told us, "*No. I don't want the treatments. If you're going to give me the treatments, just shoot me now. I want to go to heaven.*" Patrick was so very, very wise. *His faith never wavered.*

Patrick was fifteen years and three months old when he was diagnosed. I found a study online, describing the life expectancy for people with NPC. There were outliers, but the average age at time of death was sixteen years, two months.

Provisions for the Journey

> Even though I walk through the valley of the shadow of death, I will fear no evil, for you are with me, your rod and your staff, they comfort me. (Ps 23:4 ESV)

Things began to move quickly at that point. God gave us all the resources we would need to walk through the valley of the shadow of death. Looking back, I see how His hand was present in everything that happened. First, He gave us a shepherd, Pastor Gary, who made himself available to our family whenever we needed him for conversations about death, dying, and heaven. Pastor Gary connected us with Stephen ministers.[2] He had a challenge in doing that. Even though we were very much alone and desperately needed help, we didn't trust people and resisted his efforts. Pastor Gary persevered until we were each assigned a Stephen minister. We also became part of a small home fellowship group. We met every other week at our home on Wednesday evenings, after Patrick went to sleep. Members of our group told Pastor Gary that stepping into our home was like walking on hallowed ground. The church, our home fellowship group, friends, and Patrick's teachers began providing meals for us.

Patrick was a social guy and had always *loved* sports, especially baseball. He was beginning to tire easily and could only walk short distances. We purchased a sporty black wheelchair so he could continue to play sports as long as possible. He transitioned from youth sports to Unified sports, a branch of Special Olympics, at his local high school. He enjoyed Unified basketball and lacrosse, even in the wheelchair. He also liked his many therapies, including music therapy, equine therapy, and adaptive swim therapy. We wanted to keep him doing the things he loved for as long as we could, so we began to look for a wheelchair van so that we could continue taking Patrick to school, as well as his appointments and therapies.

We received three special Bibles about that time. One was a children's Bible with colorful pictures, given by a friend. The second was an "Action Bible," from our youth pastor. The third Bible was from Pastor Gary who wrote a special inscription to Patrick inside the front cover. He listed his life verses and highlighted them. We read from the Bibles daily and listened to contemporary Christian music sent to us by a family member. Patrick fell asleep in our arms each night, praying and hearing the Word of God.

God quickly connected us with the Butterfly Program, a palliative/hospice care program for children with life-limiting illnesses, at Children's Hospital. They provided us with counseling services and weekly nurse visits to our home. We started having difficult, but much-needed, conversations about death and planning for death. The work was facilitated by Suzanne Cast, the Butterfly Program's social worker. In her interactions with our family, Suzanne modeled for us the valuable lesson of how to balance intense grief work with humor. We chose to always be direct with Patrick. We promised that we would do our best to find answers to all his questions. If we didn't have the answers, we promised to be honest about that, too. I rarely left Patrick's side. I only felt safe leaving Patrick with Steve, Pastor Gary, and two families who were comfortable in handling a seizure. That summer, while Patrick hung out with his friend Mathew, Steve and I picked out our family burial spot and our gravestone. Patrick helped plan his own funeral. He told us he wanted people to wear bright colors, camo, or Western wear.

It was surreal, watching Patrick slowly fade away. We knew the end was coming, but we didn't know when. As each change would happen, I would ask our hospice nurses if the end was near. They would tell me that things were going to get worse. Each time I couldn't imagine what "worse" could look like. I grieved the loss of each part of Patrick and learned that what we were experiencing was called anticipatory grief. Steve and I also learned that men and women grieve differently. Steve held his grief inside and began to develop serious health issues. I shared my grief more openly but ate like crazy to deal with my pain. We both stopped exercising and gained *a lot* of weight. Journaling helped me process my feelings and record details of our NPC journey. The never-ending stress and fear of the unknown began to put strain on our marriage, which was already fragile.

We knew that Patrick would have more and more difficulty walking as his disease progressed, so we researched how to modify our home. We would need to put in a ramp for access to the front door. At least one bathroom would need to be made wheelchair accessible. The curved staircase was the scariest thing for us. Its wooden railing starting on the second floor at the top of the stairs reminded me of the breakaway railings that were in the old Western TV shows that Patrick loved to watch. He was big and strong. Patrick would try to get up and walk at the end of his seizures, but he would not be aware of his surroundings. I was often home alone when he had a seizure, and I wanted desperately to keep him safe. When Patrick had a seizure at the top of those stairs, I felt it was time to consider moving.

We sold our home in town and moved to a house in the country that was truly a gift from God. It was peaceful and quiet. Everything was all on one level, and Patrick would be safe. It would only need a short ramp and bathroom modifications. The house and barn sat on a few acres, so we could care for horses from DHOH. That would bring us tremendous joy. The only downside was that the property had been seriously neglected. It needed lots of work. We would tackle that a little bit at a time. We affectionately named it the Faded Rose Ranch. Sadly, our move took us out of the Butterfly Program's service area, and we needed to find new hospice provider. We worked with the Butterfly Program for several months before making a seamless transition to Denver Hospice.

The same month that we moved, we took a Make-A-Wish trip to Florida. Our team at Children's Hospital had encouraged us to take the trip sooner rather than later. Make-A-Wish Colorado pulled the trip together quickly. Patrick had heard about a coral reef restoration project in Florida. He also wanted to swim with dolphins, like his friend Max had done, so we combined activities at the Mote Research Lab and the Dolphin Research Center into one amazing trip based out of Key West, Florida. God's timing was perfect, as we would not have been able to have made the trip even one month later, due to Patrick's declining health. It was a wonderful time together as a family before things got increasingly difficult.

Lost in Space and Time

Patrick seemed lost in space and time in the days following our Make-A-Wish trip. His angels were working overtime. One day, Patrick was so excited to see his friends at school that he stood up while on the school bus's wheelchair lift. He did not fall, thank goodness. He came home from school one afternoon and asked me when the limo was coming to pick us up for our adventure in Florida. He didn't remember that we had already gone on our trip. I began praying that he would never know how much he had lost and was losing.

Patrick started to fall more often, but he didn't want to sit down while he was getting dressed. His balance and spatial awareness were going away. He also began to have difficulty swallowing. We used thicker liquids, which seemed counter-intuitive, but it helped prevent choking. He also was having difficulty speaking. The chaplain from the Butterfly Program suggested that we obtain a talking device and record his voice because we knew that some NPC kids lost their ability to speak entirely. Those precious recordings became treasures to us.

Patrick didn't complain about what was happening, but he became more and more angry. He was unable to express himself, and he lashed out. We increased his medication to help keep us safe. One night he said he wanted to die. The most dangerous times were between three and seven p.m. His symptoms were like those of Alzheimer's patients who experience late day confusion and agitation, known as sundowning. In desperation, I reached out to the National Niemann-Pick Foundation and our local Alzheimer's Association for help. We learned to turn all the lights on and cover the windows before the sun went down. Something about the shadows was upsetting to him. I don't know exactly what was happening to his vision, but his depth perception seemed to be going away. I felt like we were losing our sweet, wonderful Patrick.

Who Knew Hay Bales Could Be So Much Fun?

Thankfully, God gave us joy along the journey. He knew how much happiness and peace horses brought to both Patrick and to me. Patrick worked with horses in two capacities. We helped care for rescue horses. He also loved his weekly equine therapy sessions. Within days after we moved onto the Faded Rose Ranch, we had two rescue horses and a donkey to care for and to love. Hercules, Montana Sky, and Sally were going to be in quarantine with us as they began to learn to trust humans. We were making sure that they hadn't picked up any diseases on the feedlot. One day, while Patrick was helping me feed them, he started throwing hay up into the air. I didn't have a camera, so I had to capture that special memory in my mind. Who knew hay bales could be so much fun?

Glimpses of Heaven

I left my half-time elementary school teaching position in December and stayed home to care for Patrick. We had a huge, cowboy-themed surprise sixteenth birthday party for him. After the party was over and the guests had gone home, we met with a nurse from Denver Hospice and made arrangements to start working with them. It was so strange to go from celebrating life to planning for death. We were glad we had put resources in place because Patrick's care quickly got challenging.

Patrick experienced a steep decline in February. He began telling us about chest pain that scared him. We had oxygen on hand and tried different types of masks, but he *hated* using it and fought us when we tried to give it to him. He had facial, hand, and foot tremors when he was tired. His peripheral vision, depth perception, and spatial awareness went away during that time. He started to have trouble regulating his body temperature. His breathing changed. We changed his schedule, decreasing his school day from five hours to a couple of hours a day. *We were told that if his rate of decline continued, he could go to heaven in two weeks to two months.*

Patrick began talking about heaven more and more. He said that his adopted grandfather, Bud, was waiting for him in heaven. Patrick saw a glimpse of heaven one morning. He talked about fish and long-boards. Patrick *loved* longboards, even though he had only tried them once, during a controlled circumstance, in occupational therapy. Patrick *couldn't wait* to get his new body. *He talked about it all the time.* Our hospice nurse, Jim Peterson, told us that many of the people he had cared for over the years had similar experiences. Patrick shared my feeling that he might go to heaven soon. I so appreciated Patrick's strong faith. He led Steve and me through that scary part of our painful journey.

Chapter Three

Our Last Spring Together

Will He Remember Me?

One day in early March, Patrick attacked Steve when he came home from work. It wasn't the first time. We had enjoyed a pleasant day, and then suddenly Patrick lunged at Steve as if he were a stranger, attacking him. I reassured Patrick that everything was okay. I said that Steve was his daddy, and he was in our home to keep us safe. Patrick calmed down and hugged Steve. I was trembling. We thought that Patrick might be trying to protect me from Steve, because he thought he was a dangerous person entering our home. I called hospice to ask them about Alzheimer's or dementia patients doing that sort of thing. I had read about such things, and I had seen it in the movies, but now it was happening to us. I started to wonder—would there come a time when Patrick wouldn't remember me?

Cookie Dough Dream

Patrick told me about a dream he had about our cat, Cookie Dough, wrestling with Sundance, another cat of ours. Cookie Dough had been important to Patrick and had died several months earlier. Patrick was upset about the dream, so, based upon what the hospice nurse had been telling us, I said that I thought the dream meant that Cookie Dough was waiting for him in heaven. Patrick said that he could not wait to go there. It was interesting to note that in sixteen years, I did not recall Patrick ever telling me about a dream of his—and now he had shared two dreams in just a week. Later that day, Patrick was laughing in the back of our wheelchair van. When I asked him why he said, "*Because heaven is going to be so amazing!*"

Many Tears

We listened to music every day. Contemporary Christian, old hymns, classical, country music—we loved it all. Patrick and I sang together in the car, and it was part of our family bedtime routine. One night, we listened to a country song by Steve Wariner called "Holes in the Floor of Heaven." It helped each of us process *a lot* of sadness. We all cried hard together. Patrick had many questions about getting to heaven and what it would be like when he got there.

That night, Patrick told us he was worried about what would happen to us after he died. We reassured him that we would all be together again one day in heaven. We also told him that we had each other and the support of our church, friends, and family. We said that we would cry *a lot* for *a long time* but, that we would be okay. We told him that he would be able to watch over us. He would be with God and many people who had loved him here on Earth. Hearing those things seemed to help him feel better. That night, it felt like his homegoing could happen soon, since he was talking about heaven so much. I didn't know that in six short months, Patrick would go home to be with his heavenly Father.

Chapter Four

Notes from Pastor Gary's Sermon— Christus Victor's Theory of Atonement

On Palm Sunday, March 20, 2016, Pastor Gary preached a powerful sermon about how faith in Jesus can overcome our fear of death. At the end of his sermon, he shared something special about our family's faith journey. The following are the notes he prepared for his sermon:

"In our society, world, and culture, we are preoccupied and enamored with winning, being the best, being victorious. We are conditioned and somewhat addicted to celebrating triumphs. We know that all too well here in Denver. Although I didn't go downtown this year, on Tuesday, February 9th, close to a million fans missed work and fought crowds and traffic to celebrate our Denver Bronco's World Championship, a Super Bowl 50 victory. Yes!

"I did make that pilgrimage with our children during one of our past championships in 1998 or 1999, so I know the lure of celebrating a triumph. Winning is a lot of fun, but it can intoxicate us and distort things when we lose.

"I was on the Broncos' sidelines with the parabolic microphone on November 15th when the KC Chiefs handed us our lunch, intercepting Peyton four times. I also was at the loss to the Raiders on December 13th. It was not pretty, and there were a lot of nay-sayers and boo birds as Brock Osweiler replaced Peyton Manning in that KC game. Now we all found ourselves a month after our Super Bowl celebration, questioning and second guessing that same manage-ment that led us to victory. We reacted to the exodus of players going to other teams for their lack of loyalty to our beloved Broncos! We are truly fickle, aren't we? Enough is never enough!

"Today, we are celebrating the triumphal entry of Jesus riding into Jerusalem on that first Palm Sunday. Jesus processed on a donkey as prophesized by Zechariah, five hundred years prior, as the exiles were returning from Babylonia to rebuild the temple.

"In Zechariah 9:9 it says, 'Rejoice greatly, Daughter Zion! Shout, Daughter Jerusalem! See, your king comes to you, righteous and victorious, lowly and riding on a donkey, on a colt, the foal of a donkey.'

"In Matthew 21:10, as part of the account of Jesus fulfilling Zechariah's prophesy, it says the entire city was stirred as he entered. The non-Jews were asking, 'Who is this?' The crowds replied, 'It's Jesus, the prophet from Nazareth in Galilee.'

"Some had heard what Jesus had done through his miracles and teaching. They were eagerly awaiting a king who would deliver them from the oppressive rule of the mighty Roman Empire. Many just enjoyed a chance to celebrate whenever a parade was coming through Jerusalem. There was a handful of his true followers who knew he was the Messiah, fulfilling Old Testament prophecies. This all changed rather quickly as Jesus was later arrested, put on trial, scorned, beaten, and humiliated to the point of death on a cross.

"That is when the evil forces of the physical realm; the Pharisees, the Romans, false teachers and the evil forces of the spiritual realm, Satan and his demons, were defeated by the *Christus Victor*, Latin for 'Christ is Victorious.'

"Let's turn to Colossians 2:13–15 which says:

> 'When you were dead in your sins and in the uncircumcision of your flesh, God made you alive with Christ. He forgave us all our sins, having canceled the charge of our legal indebtedness (penal substitution), which stood against us and condemned us; he has taken it away, nailing it to the cross. And having disarmed the powers and authorities, he made a public spectacle of them, triumphing (victory in the NLT) over them by the cross.'

"This passage by Paul to the Colossians, illuminates the truth of the Theory of Atonement called

Christus Victor, that Jesus's substitutionary death on the cross bore our sin and guilt on our behalf, which gives us the incredible victory over the damnation that we rightfully deserve. In taking our place on the cross, he broke open the gates of hell, demolished the law that rightly separates us from a Holy God, destroyed the stain of sin in our lives, and freed us to walk in newness of life with God. This is all through the sacrificial death and victorious resurrection of His only begotten Son. Thanks be to God!

"Who were the powers and authorities disarmed by Jesus? Several suggestions have been made, but I believe it could be an all-inclusive list. They could be demonic powers or the gods of powerful nations, angels (which were more highly regarded than Jesus by heretical teachers in Colossae at that time), or it could be referring to the government of Rome. Jesus's death on the cross brought triumph over it all, including freedom from the power and bondage of our sin.

"Galatians 2:20 (ESV), that Pastor Doug Resler spoke of last week reads, 'I have been crucified with Christ and I no longer live, but Christ lives in me. The life I now live in the body, I live by faith in the Son of God, who loved me and gave himself for me.' It's not just about you and me, we, fortunately, are just a part of God's cosmic redemption through his Son's atoning death on the Cross!

"Next, let's look at what the author of Hebrews says in chapter 2, verses 14 and 15, that best describe this freedom through Christus Victor's view of atonement:

'Since the children have flesh and blood (each of us), he too shared in their humanity (the incarnation of Jesus, fully God, fully man) so that by his death he

25

might break the power of him who holds the power of death—that is, the devil—and free those who all their lives were held in slavery by their fear of death.'

"I recently read in my devotional by Pastor Nicky Gumbel, who started and leads Alpha Ministries in England, where he says, 'A free person is not afraid to think about death. It has been suggested, that ultimately, all your fears are related to the fear of death. In setting you free from death and the fear of death, Jesus has set you free, potentially, from all your other fears.'[3] The defeat of the devil means the setting free of those he had sway over those who had been gripped by the fear of death. Fear is an inhibiting and enslaving thing; and when people are gripped by the ultimate fear—the fear of death—they are in cruel bondage.

"Eugene Peterson says in *The Message* of these same passages in Hebrews 2:14–15.

> 'Since the children are made of flesh and blood, it's logical that the Savior took on flesh and blood in order to rescue them by his death. By embracing death, taking it into himself, he destroyed the Devil's hold on death and freed all who cower through life, scared to death of death.'

"This is freedom, brothers and sisters, living the victorious Christian life because of *Christus Victor*! If death has a hold on you, it may be an indication you've never met the one who liberates us of our sin, who defeated Satan's spiritual power of darkness and evil, and who has conquered the grave through his death on the cross and resurrection. That is why Easter is such a joyful celebration for those of us that believe in Jesus, the Messiah!

Patrick's Story

"A little over a year ago, a mom called into our office and asked if one of the pastors could meet with her and her fifteen-year-old son to talk about death and heaven. I told Vicki I would be happy to meet with them. You see, Patrick Zimmermann, had just lost a horse named Hope, that he was caring for. Hope was a rescue horse that he had worked with, and he had questions about death and heaven that Mom needed some extra help to explain to her son. So, on Sunday, March 22nd, we met for an hour or so at the Fika Coffee Shop on Main Street. We were in the middle of a series at the time here at PEPC called, "The Afterlife," so the answers to some of Cindy and Patrick's questions were fresh in my mind. It came to a point where I asked Patrick if he'd ever given his heart to Jesus and would he like to know that when he died, he would enjoy the presence of God forever. He responded that he would like to start that relationship with Jesus. We prayed around a table with many tears flowing over the joy of our time together and for Patrick's decision. I told him we were having a baptism on Palm Sunday the following week and asked if he would be interested in being baptized. I just happened to have a handout from the class we had that morning, and I gave them the information.

"He and Cindy said they would think about it and get back to me. Cindy called a day or so later to thank me for our special time together. She told me that Patrick was having some physical and mental difficulties and that the doctors at Children's were doing a battery of tests to determine his condition. She also told me that he recently had some seizures so that if we could baptize him without being immersed, Patrick would like to be baptized on Palm Sunday. She also shared that her husband Steve, who was an unbeliever, was concerned that we might embarrass his son as a part of the baptism. I reassured her that we would be very careful and thoughtful about Patrick's condition and in no way would we embarrass him.

"Palm Sunday came, and we had three others come to get baptized that Sunday besides Patrick. They each picked out a scripture to share. John Neininger, one of our deacons, a neighbor and a close friend to the Zimmermann's, came alongside Patrick and shared his verse for him.

"It was Isaiah 40:29–31, 'He gives strength to the weary and increases the power of the weak. Even youths grow tired and weary, and young men stumble and fall; but those who hope in the Lord will renew their strength. They will soar on wings like eagles; they will run and not grow weary, they will walk and not be faint.'

"Interestingly enough, we had just sung the song 'Everlasting God' before the baptism, and unbeknownst to us, those passages were in that song, which really touched Patrick deeply, as tears of joy dripped down his cheeks and everyone's who was close to him.

"Here's an observation: I think that it's amazing that with all that God is doing in people's lives in our church recently, we had no one respond to the invitation to get baptized today. After I tell the rest of Patrick's story, I think you'll know why.

"Since that special day a year ago, the Zimmermanns rarely miss a service, including Patrick's dad, Steve. In May, the family asked if I would join them at Children's Hospital as they met with several specialized doctors to discuss Patrick's condition. Cindy and Steve asked if I would open and close those sessions in prayer. It was a very humbling, yet honoring and sacred place to join their family.

"That day Patrick was diagnosed with a rare, incurable, terminal disease called Niemann-Pick Type C, a genetic disease, often referred to as Childhood Alzheimer's. I was in the room when this was told to everyone including Patrick. I then took Patrick to the cafeteria, and we sat in the garden area and talked about what he heard the doctors tell him. He said, without an inkling of fear, 'I get to go to heaven; that's awesome!' In the meantime, Steve and Cindy were given information by the doctors for palliative and experimental care options and were informed what to expect. They were told that few people lived beyond adolescence with this rare disease. That day my faith grew because of my new friend's deep faith in Christ and his hope of heaven, that continues to only get stronger with each new day. Patrick has no fear, but he does have questions from time to time like, "How is this going to happen, going from Earth to heaven? Will I ever be alone? Are my mom and dad going to be all right without me?"

"He is so excited about leaving his old broken body, his earth-suit, behind and claiming his new heavenly body, that God will provide him in heaven, and he gets to see and be with Jesus.

"Christus Victor has made himself known to Patrick. His faith this past year is rubbing off on many people. February 29th was Rare Disease Day. Since Patrick loves camo, the Legend SPED team (Special Education Department) and many of the administrators wore camo that day. Several of the staff, Shelly Boyd and Stacey Hough, are a part of our church family. Patrick is an avid sports fan and has played Unified lacrosse, so, this past Wednesday, the Legend lacrosse team named him honorary captain. When the Harlem Wizards were in town, they honored Patrick and many of his friends. Patrick has a contagious love and it's impacting others for Christ.

Steve's Story

"Probably the most significant impact happened around the same time Denver won the Super Bowl. One night after Steve tucked his son into bed at their new home near Elizabeth, Steve surrendered his heart to Jesus. The childlike, but real faith of his son, and his wife's faith through this difficult journey brought him to a place of need and belief in Jesus.

"Patrick and his mom went through the most recent Discover PEPC class, which has become their home fellowship group, that meets regularly at the

Zimmermann's home. Steve has been going to this current Discover PEPC class and recently signed up to use his electrician skills as a part of a new PEPC Men's Outreach, the Handyman Ministry.

"I'll never forget last June on Father's Day, seeing Steve and Patrick in the back row of PEPC. Upon greeting them, Steve said to me, this is 'I Sunday,' we went to IHOP for breakfast, we're here for 'I Pray' at PEPC, and then we're going to IMAX to watch a movie. God tenderized me that day, because I knew that it might be Steve and Patrick's last Father's Day together here on earth. But now, knowing of Steve's decision to trust in Jesus, I know it won't be their last; they will have many more together in eternity.

"Church family, this is the hope we have in heaven through our victorious Lord, Savior and King, Jesus the Christ, to all who believe. Amen? What does your faith in Jesus look like? Does it drown out your fear of life today, your fear of death tomorrow?

"My encouragement today, is that if you have never trusted Jesus with every part of your heart, mind, and soul, like Patrick did a year ago, today is the day of salvation, the day of triumph, the day of victory.

"We will have elders up front to pray with you. If the Holy Spirit is prompting you, let Christus Victor save you today. Let's pray."

Chapter Five

A Gift of Time

What Day Is It?

"Just so, I tell you, there is joy before the angels of God over one sinner who repents" Luke 15:10 (ESV).

After the Palm Sunday service, when Pastor Gary talked about our family's journey of faith, someone told me that there was rejoicing in heaven because Steve had come to know the Lord. Hearing that brought tears to my eyes.

Patrick continued to talk about heaven almost every day. He had a dream about Hope, the rescue horse whose death brought him to Jesus, running free in heaven. In early April we trudged through an exhausting day. We had an occupational therapy appointment in one location and two doctor appointments for Patrick in two other locations with a lot of driving in between. Meanwhile, Steve was going to his own doctor's appointment because he was dealing with serious health challenges. A member of our home fellowship group went with him, since I couldn't go along to ask all the questions that I had.

During one of the appointments, I figured out that Patrick was losing his peripheral vision. He could not see the doctor when she came up to his wheelchair from the side. We had suspected that. His depth perception was gone. His spatial awareness was gone. He also didn't know what day it was. I knew that already, because he always asked me, but it ripped my heart out to hear him say it was Tuesday, when it was actually Wednesday. I couldn't hide my feelings, and he could see dismay written all over my face. The look in his eyes will stay with me forever. The neurologist noticed other changes with his swallowing and breathing. I told the doctor about a couple of recent choking incidents. He was having difficulty regulating his body temperature. Our last appointment was with a doctor who was prescribing medicine to keep us all safe.

The only bright part of the day was that Patrick's sense of humor and flirtatious nature were still well intact. Even though he was exhausted, he turned on the charm for the nurses.

We did not schedule future appointments with the physicians. That was sobering because we had always scheduled appointments well in advance. Our hospice nurse would now keep in contact with our team of doctors for us, so we would not have to make so many treks to the hospital. We would only go in to see a doctor if it was absolutely necessary.

God's Plan, Not Mine

Pastor Doug's sermon on Sunday, April 17 at PEPC touched my heart. In it he talked about God's plan for each of us. He quoted Psalm 139:13–16.

> For you created my inmost being; you knit me together in my mother's womb. I praise you because I am fearfully and wonderfully made; your works are wonderful, I know that full well. My frame was not hidden from you when I was made in the secret place, when I was woven together in the depths of the earth. Your eyes saw my unformed body; all the days ordained for me were written in your book before one of them came to be.

I needed to hear those words. To be honest, I was struggling. The weight of watching Patrick die, ever so slowly, and growing concerns about Steve's health were overwhelming me. I needed God's reassurance. There were times I just felt like I was drowning. I was always on guard for seizures, and I was desperate for sleep. It may sound crazy, but sometimes I felt like the evil one was in my car with me, telling me to just crash the car and end it all. I had a counselor who was willing to talk with me over the phone when Patrick was asleep. She was helpful for a time, but then I asked Pastor Gary to connect me with a Christian counselor.

I was hoping to find solid biblical teaching to help me. I didn't understand why God was letting Patrick die. After surviving a painful childhood, all I wanted in life was a happy family. I couldn't understand why God was taking that away from me. I carried a well-worn card with a Bible verse that Pastor Gary had given us. I read it over and over, especially on the days I was worried about *both* Steve *and* Patrick. It said, "Do not be anxious about anything, but in every situation, by prayer and petition, with thanksgiving, present your requests to God. And the peace of God, which transcends all understanding, will guard your hearts and your minds in Christ Jesus" (Phil 4:6-7).

After being warned that Patrick might not make it to April, he seemed to be on a plateau of sorts. His new medicine was helping him sleep better, so we were having safer days. His speech became easier to understand. Unfortunately, his choking and vomiting episodes were increasing, so we steered him to foods that were easier to swallow. His breathing had changed, and I began hearing noises in his throat, even when he was sitting up. He tired easily. He needed to rest after his shower each morning. He rested for most of the day, either on the couch, if we were at home, or in his wheelchair, if we were in the community. We had switched from a regular wheelchair to a chair with a higher back to support his head.

He would forget or resist using his walker in the house. He got out of breath just walking the few steps from the kitchen to the couch. We started using a gait belt because he was unsteady. Promise Ranch Therapeutic Riding Center had graciously given us two colorful fabric gait belts. Each day, Patrick chose the one he wanted to wear for the day. The fabric gait belt gave me something to grab onto if I needed to stabilize him. His gait had changed to a stiff, Frankenstein-like walk, with his feet barely skimming the floor. His wrists were curved, and his feet were arched. I figured that his loss of peripheral vision was what caused him to miss or fall out of our dining room chairs. I stayed by his side whenever he was awake.

I held him when he was sleeping. He had yet another dream and was crying in his sleep. When I woke him, he said, "I need to give hope to others." I took comfort in knowing that Patrick's childlike, yet very real journey of faith was prompting others to think about and talk about their own personal relationships with Jesus. I asked friends to pray for us and to share Bible verses that they found particularly meaningful to them. I prayed fervently that I could learn to trust God's plan and His timing for our lives.

Pepperoni Kisses

Patrick was so affectionate to us on the good days. One night, while eating a yummy pepperoni pizza given to us by one of our dear friends, he stopped eating just long enough to give me a kiss on each cheek. What a precious memory. We could have a good, happy, and safe six hours each day, if we were careful to maintain a sleep and medication schedule. Patrick was sleeping eighteen hours a day, including a two-to-three-hour nap at midday. We cut back his school attendance to fifty minutes, twice a week. Our days were filled with therapies, school, and resting.

Patrick *hated* his seizure medicines. We did everything we could to conceal the taste, but they were nasty-tasting. Sometimes he would beg us to stop giving him the medicine so that he would have a seizure and die. I prayed that he would die peacefully and not in the middle of a scary seizure.

He had some scary choking episodes. Our hospice nurses told us to let him eat whatever brought him joy. We encouraged him to take small drinks and eat smaller bites. I had him stop eating and drinking at least a half hour before he rested. We used pillows to prop him up. He began choking on his saliva. We eventually got a special bed that we could raise and lower as we needed to keep him comfortable. We also purchased a baby monitor with a camera, so we could keep an eye on him if we were not in the room with him.

His blood pressure was steadily rising, and his oxygen levels were dropping. Sometimes his breathing was so shallow that it scared me. He had periods of several seconds when he didn't breathe. I was told that was common in hospice patients. I held him while he napped. Sometimes I held him for most of the night. We were blessed that people brought us meals, so that I could just snuggle him and not worry about cooking.

Yearning for Perfect Peace

"You will keep in perfect peace those whose minds are steadfast, because they trust in you" (Is 26:3).

Patrick and I attended an all-school assembly at Patrick's high school. He, the kids in his special needs class, and the student body at Legend High School watched a video created by two Legend students. The purpose of the video was to help students become aware of how hurtful the word *retarded* was to special needs students. The auditorium, which had been filled with rowdy students, became quiet when the powerful and moving video played. It was followed by skits performed by small groups of students. Sadness washed over me because it was so difficult to be surrounded by healthy, neurotypical kids. I sat near Patrick and pasted a happy smile on my face when I saw the baseball players in their uniforms preparing for their performance.

The enormity of Patrick's losses hit me hard. While everyone else watched the skits, I thought about Patrick's decline. Patrick had played baseball. His physical decline had started to show when he moved from coach-pitch to kid-pitch. *But he loved the game.* He had put his uniform on at six in the morning, even if the game was at two in the afternoon. Those who knew Patrick when he was young, could attest to the fact that he seemed very much like a typical kid.

His amniocentesis had showed something unusual, but no one had known what that was. He was sensitive to light and sound and a little clumsy, but he had hit all his milestones. Pediatricians never suspected anything. School became difficult, and we started asking questions in fourth and fifth grade. Seizures started in middle school. Then, the genetic testing began. Patrick had started to spend time in the Significant Support Needs (SSN) room in eighth grade. His friends in the SSN classroom were the most loving, caring young people Patrick had ever known. When he had a sixty-point drop in his IQ scores, our search for answers became urgent.

Patrick didn't say he was sad about not being able to do the things he used to do. He talked about how much he wanted a new body in heaven, so that he could longboard there. I missed sitting in the rain and snow at his sporting events. I missed doing Taekwondo with him. I missed riding bikes with him. I missed listening to him play the piano. Patrick used to talk about getting married and having a family. He was sad that he would not have a girlfriend or a wife. It was selfish, but I was so sad that I would never hold grandchildren of my own.

I listened to the song, "Perfect Peace" by Laura Story over and over. I prayed that we would continue to trust in God's plan and rely on His perfect peace.

Patrick and Hope. Natalie McElmeel, Shelly Farrell, and
Sande Nokes were also helping care for the horses.
Photo Credit Jacqui Avis

Patrick loved baseball. Photo Credit Lori A. Brundage

Patrick and Cindy. Photo Credit Steve Martin

Family Photo. Photo Credit Collette Susman,
Rustic Knot Photography

Patrick's Baptism. Pictured with John Neininger and
Max Cahill. Photo Credit Erin Funk

Participating in sports brought Patrick so much joy. The students at Legend High School were so supportive of Patrick as he declined. Back Row from left to right: Sean Theeke, Tyler Forbes, Mitchell O'Connor, Spencer LaPorte, Nastiya Matthews, Bella Kirshner, Ryan Melahn, Nathan Melahn, Jeremy Dorr. Front Row from left to right: Shelly Boyd, Dylan Secrist, Patrick Zimmermann, ShaMari Scott, Anisa Whincop, Brianna Cordova, Lauryn Dole, Taylor Mathewson. Photo Credit Scott Boyd

Patrick with Yetti.
Photo Credit Cindy Kay Zimmermann

Patrick was known for giving two thumbs up. You can see how NPC affected his hands. Photo Credit Jeremy Dorr

Patrick and Justin Kulinski. Photo Credit Allyson Kulinski

Cindy and Patrick at the Faded Rose Ranch.
Photo Credit Terry Bickel

Patrick and Mathew Campbell at Patrick's surprise 16th
birthday party. Photo Credit Cindy Kay Zimmermann

Patrick and Grace Jackson with Fancy Pants and Serendipity.
Photo Credit Grace Jackson

Patrick in water therapy with Terry Bickel.
Photo Credit Steve Zimmermann

The Zimmermann Family. Photo Credit Collette Susman,
Rustic Knot Photography

Cindy and Steve's reaffirmation of faith with Pastor Gary and
Pastor Doug. Photo Credit PEPC

Patrick. Photo Credit Steve Martin

Cindy and Steve's vow renewal officiated by Pastor Gary.
Also pictured: Meg Paige, Bob Paige, and Spencer Prince.
Photo Credit Collette Susman, Rustic Knot Photography

Cindy with Steve in Cazale, Haiti. Photo Credit Ryan Selvius

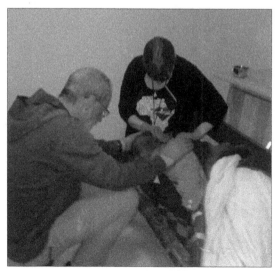

Praying with Doug Boone in Gojo, Ethiopia.
Photo Credit Steve Zimmermann

Cindy, Steve, Pastor Gary, and his wife,
Debi McCusker. Photo Credit Collette Susman,
Rustic Knot Photography

Chapter Six

May

To Board or Not to Board, That Is the Question

One of Patrick's favorite classes in middle school was drama. No surprise there. He was always a ham sandwich, loved being on stage, performing piano solos, and so forth. Patrick talked about getting a new body and longboarding in heaven *a lot.* The morning of May 1, out of the blue, complete with hand gestures, he began dramatically saying, "To board... or not to board...that is the question." When Patrick was in middle school, he had changed the words from Hamlet's soliloquy, "To be or not to be" for an assignment. Doctors had told us that we would have islands of the old Patrick appear from time to time. I wasn't sure what brought the words out that morning, but it was delightful to see a glimpse of the funny, smart, playful Patrick.

Angels Watching Over Me

On May 3, Patrick told me he saw an angel in his bedroom. He saw it two times in the same spot. Once was in the morning. He pointed to the corner of the room for a long time. The second time was when he awoke from a three-hour nap. I had held Patrick and rested with him a lot that day. He'd been tired since attending his adopted Grandma Wilma's funeral at the end of April. Wilma and her husband Bud had been neighbors of ours when Patrick was young. Patrick didn't have any living grandparents and they didn't have children of their own, so they "adopted" us and enjoyed watching Patrick grow up.

I talked with the hospice nurse and she told me that children who are dying often see angels, Jesus, or others who have passed. That conversation helped me understand why, that same week, Patrick had told me he had seen Wilma's husband, Bud, who had died ten years earlier. I told Patrick that he could see things that I couldn't see because he was closer to going to heaven than I was. I remembered a song we had sung when Patrick was young about angels watching over us.

Noisy Silence

One night in early May, I went outside to check on one of our new rescue horses, as Patrick was falling asleep in Steve's arms. While grooming Serendipity, I saw the first Indian paintbrush blooming next to one of the abundant yucca plants. I listened to the frogs singing and the red-winged blackbirds calling.

I inhaled sweet fragrance from dusky pink blossoms on the crabapple tree that was buzzing with bees. I thanked God for the Faded Rose Ranch. *Its noisy silence will help us heal*, I thought.

I noticed Patrick was eating and drinking less and less each day. Just that afternoon, he had ordered his usual meal at Sonic and only ate a small part of it. The hospice nurse had told us to go ahead and let him order food, even if he didn't eat it all because looking forward to the meal brought him pleasure.

I pondered the meaning of Dylan Thomas's poem, "Do Not Go Gentle into That Good Night." I believed that Patrick would be with Jesus in heaven when he died, so I wasn't railing against the thought of his death. I also knew that Steve and some of our dear friends were praying for a miracle. As for me, I was praying that Patrick would have a peaceful transition, not a horrific seizure or a scary death where he was struggling to breathe.

Is There Turndown Service in Heaven?

One morning, Patrick awoke after being in bed for several hours and asked, "Are there beds in heaven? I'm so tired." We contacted Pastor Gary, our resource for answers about heaven. His answer gave Patrick comfort. He responded, "That is a great question. Patrick's new perfect heavenly body won't need much rest, but I'm sure it's a five-star setup when he does." I thought to myself that Patrick would probably be expecting turndown service with candy on the pillow, like we had on our wonderful Make-A-Wish trip to Key West, Florida in October.

Patrick was now in bed for about fourteen hours each night. He woke a couple of times during the night to drink Powerade and use the bathroom. Each time he awoke, I held him to help him get back to sleep. If we kept our nighttime routine of giving medication at four p.m., followed by Bible reading, quiet music, and sleep, we all stayed safe. If Patrick got overtired, then we saw scary aggression. Fatigue also lowered his seizure threshold. We didn't want another seizure. I wanted to keep doing the activities that Patrick loved, for as long as we could. It was a delicate balancing act.

Is the Angel Here Because I'm Dying?

Patrick's mental processing time slowed dramatically in early May. It took him a long time to answer a question. Sometimes he lost track of what he was trying to say in mid-thought. When he was tired, his speech was almost unintelligible. He was falling often.

Patrick asked me one morning, "Is the angel here because I'm dying?" We were lying in his bed, talking about how his body, his earth-suit, was changing— slowing down—not working as well. He had noticed that the nailbeds of his toes were changing color and his feet were cold more and more often. I reminded him that he would get a new body in heaven and hearing that seemed to make him feel better. I asked him how seeing the angel made him feel. He said the angel made him feel safe and a little nervous. We joked that we felt like we needed to be on our best behavior, because there was an angel watching us. He didn't see the angel all the time, but it was always in the same place.

Then Patrick looked at me with a totally serious expression and said, "I think I might die today." A couple of minutes later, he said with a grin, "Nope. Not today." His sense of humor was still very much intact. Looking back, I realize that our best conversations were often in the morning when he was rested. One night, Patrick asked me if the angel could stay with him all the time. I told him that Dora Mueller, our hospice nurse, had said that some of her patients had talked to the angels they had seen, so he could ask the angel to stay until Jesus took him home.

Longing to Be in Heaven

One morning I used my perfected method of sleep-walking to the barn in the dark, while Steve stayed inside with Patrick, in case he awoke. The air and grass outside were heavy with moisture. Morning dew gently caressed my cheek, waking me slowly. I sleepily fed grain to the horses as I did each day. Freedom, an older Arabian mare who came to us from Wyoming, where she had been starved, was having trouble holding her weight, so I gave her senior grain. A rooster crowed as I headed back to the house.

I typed a journal entry as a delicate pinkish orange washed the sky, heralding the sun's arrival. Patrick stirred, so I tried to snuggle him back to sleep. He was restless and unsettled, just as he had been earlier that night. The music that usually calmed him had instead thrown him into a rage. We also had had a rough couple of hours between 12:45 and 2:30 a.m. Patrick was having facial tremors, body tics, and phantom itches. We didn't know if they were surface-level or deep tissue, but the itches made him frustrated.

My sleep-deprived brain had compared Patrick's restlessness to a butterfly. I wondered, *Is Patrick struggling to escape his earth-suit, like a butterfly escaping its chrysalis?* I knew I was anthropomorphizing, but it made me wonder what a butterfly felt as it worked to break out of its chrysalis. I thought of the words of John Gillespie Magee Jr.'s poem, "Oh! I have slipped the surly bonds of Earth and danced the skies on laughter-silvered wings."[4]

I wondered, *Does a butterfly long to dance the skies as Patrick longs to be in heaven?* Patrick couldn't always express what he was feeling, but he showed us by raging. At 1:30 a.m., he had tried to forcibly remove the SuperPole installed next to his bed to help him stand up and sit down. I convinced him to take extra medicine at 2 a.m. to help him calm down. I had kept Patrick safe. I came away from the night with only a sore wrist. I prayed that we would continue to be able to keep Patrick and ourselves safe.

Watch the Animals

Jim, one of our hospice nurses, suggested that we watch the animals in our home to tell us when changes were happening with Patrick. While helping Patrick get to sleep one night, I noticed both of our cats sitting close together at the foot of Patrick's bed. That was unusual because Blaze and Sundance didn't usually get along. Having made peace, they sat together and listened to classical music with the three of us as Patrick drifted off to sleep. Sundance, our dog-wannabe, also seemingly attempted to comfort Patrick whenever he was upset. He would climb onto Patrick's chest when he was lying in bed. This distracted Patrick and helped him let go of any idea or object on which he was perseverating. I noticed Sundance also followed Patrick around the house, winding through his legs each time he sat down. He slept on Patrick's bed most nights.

A Cowboy's Last Trail Ride?

"To everything there is a season, and a time to every purpose under the heaven" (Eccl 3:1 KJV).

On May 14, Patrick's wonderful therapeutic riding instructor, Shannon, made special arrangements so that Patrick could ride Yetti outside, something he *loved* to do. Shannon made sure the other horses stayed in their stalls and were not outside, so that Patrick could safely cross a trickling stream and explore the pastures surrounding Promise Ranch. Patrick was well-supported for his therapeutic riding. He had two side walkers who each kept a hand on him and watched him while he was riding, in case he was to have a seizure or feel weak and start to fall. Shannon also led Yetti. Patrick said riding Yetti was like riding a tan sofa. Yetti was a Norwegian Fjord horse who seemed to love Patrick. I followed along, as usual, snapping photographs.

I think Patrick enjoyed joking around with Shannon and the helpers. He even might have been showing off a little for the pretty side walker with long, blonde hair. He rode for a long time, but when he went to dismount at the ramp, he leaned over and seemed exceptionally weak.

Patrick fell asleep in the van before we even got out of Promise Ranch's driveway. When we got home, he visited with my family for a bit before taking an extra-long nap. Then he went to bed early and had an unsettled night. I wondered if Patrick had ridden his last long trail ride. I thought how sad it would be to stop doing the things that he loved to do. I prayed that we would have the wisdom to listen to what Patrick was telling us without words.

Lord, I Am Weary

We had several aggressive episodes within a couple of days. "Lord, I am weary. Please give me strength and patience," I prayed. Patrick slept through one night until three a.m. Blessed sleep. Unfortunately, when I went to snuggle with him to help him get back to sleep, I was greeted with a fist. Apparently, my elbow was touching him. He apologized. It was so hard to go from snuggling to fight-or-flight and back to loving Mom again in just a couple of minutes.

I got Patrick back to sleep and then trudged to the barn. Nickers from hungry horses were such a sweet sound. They were accompanied by a chorus of birds greeting the day. Fog hugged the ground like a blanket—remnants of the previous day's rain showers. The mist made me think of a piano solo called "The Highlands of Scotland" composed by Mary Leaf, that Patrick had played with such sensitivity when he was much younger.

I prayed that we would have the wisdom to adjust Patrick's medication as we needed to stay safe, but I didn't want to overmedicate him and lose the fragments of Patrick's personality that we had left.

Crash Course in Christianity

"God began doing a good work in you, and I am sure He will continue it until it is finished when Jesus Christ comes again" (Phil 1:6 NCV).

"Submit yourselves, then, to God. Resist the devil, and he will flee from you" (Jas 4:7).

Some dear Christian friends we had been blessed to know for many years, told us that our family was taking a crash course in Christianity. They were right. I knew they had prayed for our family for a long time, and we so appreciated those prayers. I knew many people were holding us up in prayer each day. I asked all our friends to pray specifically for our protection.

PEPC had wrapped their arms around our family in ways too many to count, showering us with blessings. They had welcomed us, strangers, into their family. I talked with believers at PEPC about the struggles we were having. I had begun thinking of the world in terms of spiritual warfare, something totally beyond my level of understanding. I was hoping my mature Christian friends would understand what I was describing. I asked for protection for our hearts and minds. As we watched Patrick decline and we faced more and more challenging behaviors caused by NPC, it felt like the devil was trying to tell us to ignore all the wonderful things with which we have been blessed, by making us return to fear, doubt, and despair.

I had prayed for years that I would share a faith with my husband. That prayer was answered. I had prayed that we would sit in worship together. That prayer had also been answered. I believed that we would all be together in heaven—another answered prayer. I knew that Patrick would have a new body in heaven. Our prayers for healing would be answered when he got to heaven.

I had personal evidence showing the power of prayer in my life. Our family was living proof that the Lord had lovingly pursued us. Psalm 23, that I had memorized as a child, served me well. I was seeing daily evidence that the Lord was walking with us through the valley of the shadow of death. A new verse I was learning from James 4:7, about resisting the devil, was also helping me cope. In the months to come, I would learn about putting on the full armor of God to protect myself from spiritual attack as I studied Ephesians 6:10.

Still, the evil one continued to try to plant seeds of despair and hopelessness in me. The devil wanted me to give up. He wanted me to go back to my old ways of thinking, feeling, and acting. I was able to fight those dark impulses, because God was doing a work in me. I was not the person I once was. I didn't ever wish to be that person again.

Rearranging Furniture

"If any of you lacks wisdom, you should ask God, who gives generously to all without finding fault, and it will be given to you" (Jas 1:5).

Our hospice team talked with us that week about meeting Patrick's needs as he declined. We talked about bringing in a hospital bed, when it became necessary. We would need to rearrange some furniture for that. We had already installed a SuperPole, a sturdy pole reaching from ceiling to floor, to help him get in and out of his bed. We also had purchased a wedge to help him sit up in bed. We were told to expect Patrick's aggression to increase as the disease took over his brain. After two peaceful months, Patrick had several bursts of aggression within a week, so we adjusted his medication. We started talking about plans for how to give him medicine when it became more difficult for him to swallow. I kept reminding myself that our sweet Patrick could not control what was happening to him, and that out-of-control feeling must be especially upsetting for him. I prayed that we would respond to the aggression with love and infinite patience and that we would have the wisdom to do what was best for Patrick's care, as his needs changed.

Higher Ground

For we know that when this earthly tent we live in is taken down (that is, when we die and leave this earthly body), we will have a house in heaven, an eternal body made for us by God himself and not by human hands. We grow weary in our present bodies, and we long to put on our heavenly bodies like new clothing. (2 Cor 5:1–2 NLT)

The Higher Ground Men's Chorus performed a concert in honor of Patrick at PEPC. What a wonderful blessing. They performed one of Patrick's favorite songs, "I'll Have a New Life," and *he loved it!* The tenors sang the part, "I'll have a new body!" *We sang that all the time* at the Faded Rose Ranch. Pastor Gary shared Patrick's story during the concert. Some dear friends of ours said that the clouds slipped away, and the sun shone brightly into the sanctuary while Pastor Gary was talking about Patrick's faith.

Staying up late for the evening concert was a challenge, but we adjusted his medication and were held in prayer for safety. Things were a little edgy, but we made it home and got Patrick to bed with few issues. Once Patrick fell asleep, I checked on the horses in the light of a nearly full, orange moon. It was surprisingly still, just a quiet chorus of frogs and a single jet flying overhead. I reflected on the events of the day. We had prayed about attending the concert, because things got dangerous if we stayed up late, but we did it! During the concert, I just let the music wash over me. It was so wonderful. It was what I imagined music would be like in heaven. I continued to be amazed as I watched how God was using our family's pain for good. People longed to know Jesus the way Patrick did. Praise the Lord!

Wildflowers Everywhere

> And why do you worry about clothes? See how
> the flowers of the field grow. They do not labor
> or spin. Yet I tell you that not even Solomon in
> all his splendor was dressed like one of these.
> (Mt 6:28–29)

Each week, we were blessed to have a kind family
stop by to help with the horses and chores at the
Faded Rose. While Steve snuggled with Patrick, I got
some work done outside with the three rescue horses
from DHOH. I thought that one of the mares, Fancy
Pants, might be pregnant. That would be exciting. I
couldn't wait to tell Patrick. Even though he couldn't
help with chores anymore, he loved to hear all the
news about the horses and watch them through the
windows in our house.

We had a new rescue, an Arabian, named
Freedom. We walked the pasture in search of her fly
mask before starting the chores. Freedom and twelve
other horses had been rescued from a neglectful
situation in Wyoming. One of Freedom's eyes was
swollen when she came to Colorado. The eye had
been bothering her again, so we were trying to get
her to wear a mask. Freedom kept taking it off and
leaving it all over the pasture. We found hidden treasures as we walked. Concealed from the road and
the fence line by large yucca plants, delicate wildflowers of white, pink, blue, orange, and yellow *were
everywhere.* Steve and I would need to help Patrick
get out to see them. I found a tiny frog under a log,
I'm not kidding, when I was cleaning up trash near

the loafing shed. Terns were swooping and calling to one another. I kept my eye out for the heron that had been stealing the Koi from our backyard tank. No sign of him.

We prayed that night again for safety and peace. We were monitoring Patrick's medication doses and making changes as needed to keep everyone safe. The hardest part about NPC for us, at that point, was the aggression. Patrick could not control what frustrated him. It came on so quickly. It had to be so upsetting for Patrick, who had been such a gentle person. It was terrifying for me, because it reminded me of times when I had been hurt by someone in a rage. I had to work hard to separate my deep emotional response from what was happening in the moment. We needed to keep Patrick and ourselves safe.

Count It All Joy

Count it all joy, my brothers, when you meet trials of various kinds, for you know that the testing of your faith produces steadfastness. And let steadfastness have its full effect, that you may be perfect and complete, lacking in nothing. Blessed is the man who remains steadfast under trial, for when he has stood the test, he will receive the crown of life, which God has promised to those who love him. (Jas 1:2–4, 12 ESV)

One morning, on our trash day, I rolled two large trash containers down our long, dirt driveway to the unpaved County Road 13. The Faded Rose had been a bank-owned property when God led us to it. We could see its hidden beauty. It required *lots* of TLC. Each week we removed some of the trash and debris. We also had a huge trailer loaded and ready to take to the dump. As I walked and listened to the morning's nature choir, featuring an owl on bass, singing from the top of the power pole, and a tenor solo by a neighbor's rooster, I pondered the words of a song called, "Count It Joy." Patrick and I listened to it on a CD by the Higher Ground Men's Chorus. I had read the same message in our daily devotional, so I figured it was a lesson I needed to learn from James 1:2–12.

I also thought it was no accident that Pastor Gary and the elders from PEPC were coming out to pray with our family that week. Patrick didn't know it, but if he continued to decline at his current rate, he would not be going back to school in the fall. I had a lot of growing to do in my spiritual maturity to be able to find joy in our NPC journey.

I thought back to 1999, when I stood in a small phone room at Franktown Elementary. I was working as a clinical professor, supervising new teachers in St. Vrain Valley Schools. In that tiny room, I learned that Patrick's amniocentesis showed something unusual. I sagged against the cold cinderblock wall that afternoon, taking in the enormity of what that might mean for our future. Niemann-Pick Type C was such a rare disease that I wouldn't know the answer for years, when we finally got a diagnosis.

I wondered, if Patrick had not had NPC and experienced the challenges that went with it, would we have become involved with DHOH? Would Patrick have met the sweet, caring cohort of special needs students at

Legend High School? Would we have become part of the wonderful, loving PEPC family? Would Patrick and Steve have become Christians? Would I have come to walk with the Lord as closely? I didn't know the answers to those questions. I prayed that we would continue to trust in God's plan for our lives as our faith was being burnished by the daily trials we faced on Patrick's NPC journey.

God's Sense of Humor

> "And even the very hairs of your head are all numbered" (Mt 10:30).

Pastor Gary and the elders from PEPC, braved an afternoon hailstorm to drive to the Faded Rose Ranch and pray over us. Patrick's illness had been creating tremendous stress in our family. We felt like the evil one had been trying to mess with us throughout each day. We knew that this kind of situation could destroy a relationship, and we wanted to have support to help our marriage stay strong, despite the hardships we faced. Pastor Gary asked God to bring us closer together and to help make our marriage stronger than it had ever been. An elder prayed with each of us and anointed our heads with oil. As one of the elders wrapped up the prayer session by telling the devil and his minions to leave our home, we heard a booming clap of thunder just outside. We all laughed a little nervously. Who says God doesn't have a sense of humor? I believed God knew every hair on my stubborn, Norwegian head, and He knew that I needed a bolt of lightning to show me *He was indeed paying attention to our situation.* He showed me just how powerful He was that day and that He would defeat the schemes of the devil to destroy my family and my marriage.

Caregiving 101

I learned a tough lesson at the end of May. I needed to take care of myself, so that I could do a good job taking care of my family. After five months of trying to do it all 24/7, I hit the wall. We were entering a challenging phase in Patrick's care. He was having more and more difficulty swallowing. He spat out his medicine. He was also falling more each day. He still wanted to walk around but didn't realize how unsteady he was becoming.

I finally asked hospice to send someone out to help with bathing because he took such a hard fall while I was getting him dressed one morning. Patrick *did not* want to sit down while dressing. He weighed close to 190 pounds, and I needed to keep him safe.

I took a bit of time for myself one evening. After Patrick fell asleep in Steve's arms, I slipped out to the garage, carefully removed a spider and her web from my pearlescent pink Pinarello bike and rode a couple of laps on the Zane Grey Loop, a paved road just two minutes from the Faded Rose. The Pinarello is the same bike I was riding when I met Steve, while we were both racing for Turin Bicycles, thirty years before. Not much had changed on that bike, and it still made me feel young. I wanted to be with Patrick every moment, but I prayed that I would be wise enough to ask for short periods of respite when I needed it.

Chapter Seven

June

Sophomore Achievement Award—A Gentle Soul with a Big Heart

Patrick was given a Sophomore Achievement Award at Legend High School as the school year ended. Since he could not stay up late, Jason Jacob, the principal, talked to him about the award during the day, and they recorded a video of that conversation to show at the ceremony. His teacher, Keri Myers, shared her script with us. Ms. Myers worked with him and had seen his dramatic decline over the last two years. Niemann-Pick had not dampened Patrick's loving spirit. We were so proud of our son.

"Hello, my name is Keri Myers and I have the distinct honor of presenting the Sophomore Achievement Award to Patrick Zimmermann, an outstanding person. Unfortunately, Patrick is unable to join us this evening. However, I would like to share a video of Patrick with you. As you can see, Patrick faces some pretty serious challenges in his life. What you won't see, is Patrick acting like a victim of these challenges. When our team describes Patrick, these are just a few of his qualities we speak of:

- Patrick is funny and kind; his smile lights up a room.
- Patrick never gives up and encourages all his friends.
- Patrick always finds the positive in any situation and has a fantastic sense of humor.
- Patrick is a very social and likable young man. He is energetic and fun-loving. Whether at school or Unified lacrosse, Patrick always brings a smile to those around him. He genuinely cares about people and has made lasting relationships. Patrick is one-of-a-kind.
- Patrick is kind to everyone and sees only the good in people. He is not selfish and thinks of others.
- Patrick is talented in any situation and has the insight to create something out of nothing. He has an infectious laugh that gets the entire class laughing about the silliest things. His sensitivity is special, and we all benefit from his kindness, when he is with us. His spirit is endearing.
- Everyone has been touched by Patrick. He is a gentle soul with a big heart. I cannot say enough about Patrick. He is very, very special and is truly is an outstanding person, so deserving of this award."

Ode on a Strawberry Rhubarb Pie

One of my favorite poems in college was "Ode on a Grecian Urn" by John Keats.

Sleep deprivation was doing funny things to my brain. As I was snuggling in the middle of the night with a softly snoring Patrick, I wondered how I could write an ode about our friend Linette's delicious strawberry rhubarb pie. She was so sweet to make Patrick's favorite pie for him. We were blessed to have delicious food from Linette and many others. Another friend brought chocolate chip cookies on a regular basis. Yum! Having food lovingly made and delivered to our home freed me to snuggle several hours a day with Patrick, which is what I loved to do. It calmed him and helped keep us all safer. We were blessed.

I continued to pray for safety. As NPC progressed, Patrick was less able to manage his frustration, and he was lashing out at me. We were told by hospice that was common in their patients. It was so painful. We also prayed that Steve would be able to focus and keep his job. He had a wonderful employer, but the stress was making it harder and harder for him to concentrate at work.

We were delighted to have a visit from Carol and Kristen, Steve's sister and her daughter. They came all the way from Georgia and Tennessee, respectively. We shared lots of laughter and tears. Carol and Kristen jumped right in and helped to keep Patrick safe, mowed the lawn, painted the chicken coop, washed dishes, folded laundry, dusted, and even baked brownies. Yummy. We also had lots of help from my sister, Judy, and her friend, Jim. They helped with sewing valances for the windows and mucking the pasture. Members of our PEPC family continued to bring meals. They were delicious. I loved being able to totally focus on snuggling with Patrick. We truly appreciated the help.

Steve was busy battling mosquitoes. We had a broken pipe in the pasture, and it created just the right environment for a mosquito habitat. The two rescue horses and mule were miserable. It took three days of digging to locate and repair the leak. That left no time for other yard work.

Carol, Kristen, Steve, and I got to participate in Patrick's weekly music therapy, which was lots of fun. As we said our goodbyes on Sunday evening, a lovely rainbow appeared along with the first shimmering hummingbird at our feeder.

Patrick started saying, "I'll meet you at the gates of heaven." I was able to record him saying that on his iPad. We were capturing his voice, because it was getting harder and harder for him to talk.

Patrick was unsteady on his feet, but he still wanted to get up and walk around, so I always needed to be ready to keep him safe. I asked friends and family to pray for his safety.

A Single Tear

Patrick did not complain about what NPC was doing to his body, but he was becoming sad more often. When he did, emotion flooded his eyes and his face. Usually, a single tear rolled down his cheek. He was losing the ability to verbalize his feelings, so I just hugged him tightly until the emotions subsided. I prayed that Patrick would know God's peace.

Patrick had a doctor's appointment Thursday at Children's Hospital. It was frustrating and exhausting. Dr. Elias was kind enough to give up her lunch/charting time in order to fit us into an already full schedule, but that meant Patrick didn't get his usual nap, and he lost it while we were at the pharmacy after the appointment. I had been concerned about Patrick's liver functioning because I knew that NPC affected the liver. As I suspected, his liver was larger than it had been at his last visit. He had blood drawn, and the nurse had difficulty finding a vein and getting enough blood for the tests. Our wonderful hospice nurse, Dora, went to the appointment with us. I knew that Patrick was dehydrated because he couldn't drink liquids easily. She explained later that Patrick's body was concentrating on sending blood to his major organs. That's why his extremities were often cold and why the nailbeds of his toes were sometimes dark in color.

We got new rescue medication for seizures, since our medicine was a year old. Our neurologist, Dr. Palat, called us at home Friday and said that seizures were likely to increase in frequency. Patrick had started having brief seizures about once a day. They only lasted a short time, but they were scary to watch, since he didn't respond to us while they were happening.

God continued to bless us and send help as we needed it. Our family was selected to receive help from a group of realtors called Helping Hands. Pastor Gary had encouraged us to apply, and we were chosen. What a godsend. We chose to buy the Faded Rose

Ranch, even though it was bank-owned and needed lots of work, because everything was on one level and was much safer for Patrick. We had planned to do all the work ourselves, but Steve started to develop serious health issues caused by stress, and he was less able to complete the work. In August, a large group of approximately sixty people would spend two days, completing needed repairs to the outside of the house and the property.

We thanked God for all our blessings. We prayed that we would be able to keep Patrick safe at home and in the community and that we would continue to trust in Jesus through the painful times ahead.

Don't Forget the Guy in the Wheelchair

Patrick was confusing reality with nonreality more and more. I pondered this while giving medicine to our rescues one morning under the light of a full moon, shining through the thin clouds left over from the previous night's thunderstorms. We had two mares and a mule staying with us. Freedom, the Arabian, had recently found a home with a loving family. I was serenaded by an owl and an oriole, leading the morning's chorus. My neighbor's Bronco growled its way up Wild Rose Circle, the dirt road on the south side of our property.

Patrick had lost his sense of time and had difficulty remembering things, so I kept our routine predictable and repetitive in an effort to help him feel safe. We watched our favorite movies and read the same books over and over. On one of our treks, Patrick was watching *Despicable Me 2*, as we often did while driving in our white wheelchair van. Excitedly he shouted at the overhead movie screen, "Don't forget the guy in the wheelchair!" I realized that he wanted to join in the dance at the end of the movie. Later in the day, we were reading *Diary of a Wimpy Kid,* as we did each afternoon. He began to copy the actions of one of the characters.

The previous summer, when we were working with the Butterfly hospice team from Children's Hospital, we began to plan Patrick's funeral. Even then, Patrick had told us he did not want people to remember him in a wheelchair. He wanted people to wear bright colors and wear Western wear to his memorial service. I had never thought of Patrick as "the guy in the wheelchair," and I was surprised that he saw himself that way. But he was spending more and more time in the chair, so I guess it made sense.

We thanked God for those who were holding us in prayer each day. We prayed that we would listen to God's leadings about how to best care for Patrick. We asked God for continued strength and peace because, sometimes the anticipatory grief washed over us in giant waves.

God's Love Personified

On June 22nd, Patrick rode Yetti at Promise Ranch. It was getting more challenging for him to mount and dismount, so things were carefully orchestrated in order to keep him safe. When he got on Yetti without incident, Elaine, one of his amazing instructors said, with relief in her voice, "That was smooth!"

Patrick paused for dramatic effect and then said with a smile, "Like butta (butter)!" His team of volunteers responded with smiles and laughter. We said that phrase—smooth like butta—a lot at home. I was so glad that Patrick's stage presence and sense of humor were still firmly intact.

Each night, we read from the Bible and a wonderful devotional called *Jesus Calling.* That night's message, drawn from Psalm 116:17 and Philippians 4:4–6, told me to thank Jesus for the things that were difficult in my life. I thought about those words as I walked around thigh-high columns of yucca flowers on my way to give a pain pill to Shakira, a crippled mule rescue from DHOH. She was a sweet gal. She was a new arrival and seemed to enjoy limping slowly around the property. I noticed that she was missing a piece of her right ear. She didn't like wearing her fly mask with a silly design on it that made her look like she had fake eyelashes and curlers. Her own eyes were soft and beautiful. I inhaled the scent of the sweet hay as I fed her. I saw beauty in the yucca blossoms. They appeared to be burgundy when tightly closed, emerging as cream, brushed with a hint of purple and pale green when they opened. My enjoyment was limited because I knew that they promised thousands more yucca plants, even as we worked to clear the acreage of the spiny yucca plants.

With my hand on Shakira, following the devotional's urging, I whispered the words, "Thank you, Lord, for Niemann-Pick." The pain I felt as I spoke almost made me nauseous because, *I realized that Patrick's disease had opened my heart.* Until he was born, I had not known that I could love anyone as much as

I loved him. Sharing Patrick's story with others had allowed me to glimpse God's love here on Earth. From the prayers of complete strangers to the loving hand holding mine in prayer, I had seen and felt God's love in ways I never even imagined. God was gently helping me learn how to trust people. I thanked God for those He had sent to walk the NPC journey with us. Their prayers and acts of kindness were God's love, personified.

Joy Comes in the Morning

The night of June 23rd was a rough one at the Faded Rose. Sundance, our sweet kitty who loved Patrick so much, started throwing up at high noon and didn't stop. Then, at four in the morning, Patrick had trouble breathing. We tried unsuccessfully to get him to use his Broncos breathing mask. Patrick also had diarrhea three separate times in the night. Early in the morning, I found yet another cat barf pile. When I told Patrick, he said with a big grin, "Remember, Mom, joy comes in the morning!" Psalm 30:5 (ESV). I told him that I sure hoped I wouldn't find any more piles of joy around here. We had sung that line with Patrick at PEPC in a song called "Your Love Never Changes" by Jesus Culture. I loved that kid. I really loved that kid. Now, if I could only get some sleep.

A Bad Day Fishin'

Patrick got to ride in a special electric off-road wheelchair at a fishing event sponsored by Outdoor Buddies. Larry Sanford and Chase Swift gave Patrick a special memory. The fish weren't biting for us, but you know what they say, "A bad day of fishin' beats a good day of anything else!"

The Angel's Back

On June 28th, Pastor Gary stopped by and prayed with our family. We were so blessed to have Pastor Gary and our PEPC family supporting us through such a challenging time. Just before he fell asleep that night, Patrick told me that he would be waiting for me at the gates of heaven. That was his new favorite thing to say as he fell asleep. On an impulse, I asked if his angel was with us. He whispered in an oh-my-goodness tone that, yes, the angel was in the room. He didn't raise his hand and point like he did the first time he saw it. This time he kept his eyes lowered. I didn't want to push because it seemed to be hard for him to talk about it. He had not talked about his angel in a couple of weeks. I was glad that the angel brought him comfort, since he had been more melancholy lately. It hurt my heart to see him sad.

The next morning, I saw Patrick have a focal seizure while he was riding Yetti. I was a side-walker, so I was standing next to him with my hand on his leg. He didn't lose his balance or fall, he just stared blankly for about eight to ten seconds. He was having that type of mini-seizure daily. When we returned home from therapeutic horseback riding, a young buck was sleeping under the shade trees in our front yard. We had fun counting the points on his antlers. We think we counted eight. That made Patrick smile. At our former home in town, we used to have deer sleeping under our deck, at mid-day, all the time. The buck watched us curiously as we parked our van and ate our lunch inside it. Then, he stood up, stretched, and moseyed up County Road 13. We had hoped to plant a garden earlier in the spring, but that would have to wait until another year. I realized that we would have to make the garden fence both rabbit-proof *and* deer-proof. I wondered if the buck had nibbled on my rosebuds.

Chapter Eight

July

Resting in God's Embrace

On July 1st, I accidentally left the house without the seizure rescue medication to be given if Patrick had a seizure lasting more than five minutes. It had been a year since Patrick had a seizure continuing that long. As we parked our wheelchair van outside of his music and massage therapy office, I jokingly said, "Okay, Patrick, I don't have your rescue medication with us, so don't have a seizure." Without missing a beat, I heard a robotic-like voice saying, "Seizure! Seizure!" Patrick pretended to have a seizure, complete with eye rolling and twitches. I just had to love that guy!

During Patrick's therapy sessions I thought about the lyrics to a song called "Oceans" by Joel Houston, Matt Crocker, and Salomon Ligthelm. The words in the song touched my heart, especially the part about my soul resting in God's embrace. Our niece, Kristen Cotter, had included that song on the Christian music CDs she sent us all the way from Tennessee. Patrick *loved* to sing along with the music on our way to his various therapies! Several people had told me recently that they thought I was strong. I knew that I was only strong because I was leaning on God. I prayed continuously that God would give me strength.

On Eagle's Wings

On July 2nd, Patrick's childhood friend, David Meyer, did something particularly special to honor Patrick's impact on his life during his Eagle Scout Court of Honor. David won an award for Outstanding Eagle Project in 2015. He presented his trophy to Patrick. It was such a caring gesture from a remarkable young man. We truly appreciated that, because it helped us to know that Patrick's life was not going unnoticed.

We prayed together before he took medicine because it was so difficult. He often choked and threw up the medicine. We talked with Patrick about how we could use the symbol of the eagle on the trophy to draw strength. He began to think of the eagle image from his baptismal verse to help him swallow his awful-tasting medicine. "He gives strength to the weary and increases the power of the weak" (Isaiah 40:29). That night, he just gulped the medicine down without hesitation.

We asked friends and family to begin thinking of and writing down the special memories they had of Patrick and the way his life and faith had impacted their lives. Hearing those stories would bring us comfort in the days to come and after Patrick went to be with Jesus in heaven. We didn't know how much time he had left on this side of heaven. I only knew that we needed to treasure each and every day that Patrick was with us.

Have Eyes but Fail to See

"Do you have eyes but fail to see, and ears but fail to hear" (Mk 8:18).

In early July, we began noticing that Patrick was slowly slipping away, even more, mentally. I talked about it with Ginny Swenson, our hospice social worker, during her weekly visit to the Faded Rose. She confirmed the subtle changes that we had been seeing day-to-day. After she left, I was thinking about our conversation while I walked all the way across the pasture to the corner where the mares were standing. I was rewarded for my trek by getting a close look at the yellow asters and Mexican hat flowers that were flourishing. Coyotes were vocalizing in the distance as they did each evening. Fancy Pants and Serendipity seemed to be watching something far off in my neighbor's grassy acreage.

I had to go back into the house and use binoculars to confirm that they were watching a large antelope herd. It was the first time I had seen antelope that close to our house. Just like I hadn't been totally sure what I was seeing in the pasture, I needed Ginny to confirm that Patrick's affect seemed to be flatter. He was taking longer and longer to respond to questions. It was hard to describe, but he seemed to be less aware of his body. He told me that the angel was with us every day now.

We purchased a new adjustable bed to help him sleep better. We could raise the head of the bed. Liquid was collecting in his throat, and we hoped the more upright position might help with his breathing. Apparently, it was more comfortable, because he slept fifteen hours straight the first night.

We continued to pray for strength as we saw the heart-wrenching changes in Patrick.

Who Ya' Callin' Shorty?

If I had written a journal entry on July 6th, it would have been titled, "What's Next—Locusts?" Thanks to singing, exercise, sleep, horse hugs, and wise counsel from our support system, when I sat down to write, I could look at things more positively. The words to the old song, "It Is Well with My Soul" by Horatio G. Spafford, brought me peace, especially the phrase comparing sorrows to rolling sea billows. I sang that song over and over.

July 6th had been an emotional rollercoaster with somber news about Steve's health and a heavy-duty discussion with Dora, our hospice nurse. We talked about responding to emergency situations that might arise when I was alone with Patrick, either at home or in the van. Patrick had been choking more and more. I had asked her to help me wrap my head around possible scenarios so that I could respond in a somewhat calm manner. I wasn't as prepared for the discussion as I had thought. Dora helped me work through some of the powerful emotions that emerged.

Wise advice I received later in the evening, included a comparison of our lives to a soda can that was jostled about all day. That analogy helped me understand why I sometimes felt like I was about to explode at the slightest provocation.

Thankfully, July 7th was filled with laughter and joy. Patrick discovered that he was tall enough to put his arm around me and kiss me on the forehead. He delighted in calling me "Shorty" all day. Later, he wanted me to blow raspberries on his belly like I did when he was young. He was very much like a small child, only in a sixteen-year-old's body. We laughed over family scrapbooks, and Patrick wanted to bite my nose, just like the picture we found of him gently biting Steve's nose when he was a baby.

Horse hugs were wonderful therapy. Serendipity always stopped grazing and wandered over to greet me. She liked attention and hugs. So did Shakira. She was standing over a spiny yucca plant one night when I gave her a pain pill hidden in a horse cookie. I noticed that the yucca's unopened seed pods were covered with insects, including ladybugs and teeny, tiny, tan grasshoppers.

I prayed that we would be able to handle whatever challenges we faced calmly, with peace in our souls.

Laughter Is the Best Medicine

"A cheerful heart is good medicine, but a crushed spirit dries up the bones" (Prv 17:22).

There was *lots* of laughter at the Zimmermann home when the Brundages came to visit. Mitchell (Mitchie) and his mom, Lori, made Patrick laugh so hard, he almost cried. Mitchie and Patrick had known one another since their youth soccer days when they played defense together and called themselves "The Wall," because nothing got past them. Mitchie had always had such wonderful comedic timing that he could have been Robin Williams's "brotha' from anotha' motha.'" Sometimes I must confess that I felt like the big, black beetle I saw bumbling along behind the barn—too wrapped up in the journey to stop and savor small precious moments of joy. Those were like little presents waiting to be opened! We loved that Mitchell and Lori gave us the gift of joy that day.

Patrick had it figured out. He was leading us along the journey just like he had from the beginning. His current favorite song was "The Best Days of My Life," by Jason Gray. He called it the bike song. It talked about God lovingly leading us home. We sang it over and over. I prayed that we would look for joy each day.

Do Cats Pray?

Patrick asked an interesting question, "Do cats pray?" We were lying on his new, amazingly comfortable, adjustable bed with Sundance stretched out at our feet. I said, "I don't know. God created us and wants us to communicate with Him, so therefore I think that since God also created animals, He must have a way for cats to communicate with Him as well." Luckily, Patrick seemed satisfied with that answer.

Patrick was getting better sleep on his new bed, so we were having better days. Praise the Lord! He also told me that there were two angels here sometimes. Steve thought one of them was here to keep an eye on me, because I had experienced some dark days clouded with worry about the future.

Our devotional, *Jesus Calling* by Sarah Young, had several entries that I think were important for me to hear. One of the most important lessons I was learning as we traveled Patrick's NPC Journey was about trust—trusting God and trusting people. We had been blessed by so many caring people that week. There had been lots of phone calls and visits. It had been like Christmas in July for Patrick. We were so grateful! It helped me to see that we were not alone on the journey. I prayed that we would learn to take things one step at a time, trusting that God would be there for us every step of the way.

Sleep is a Wonderful Thing

In mid-July Patrick caught a cold. His nose was stuffy. His ears were full. He was miserable and irritable. He refused to use oxygen. Even with his new bed, Patrick couldn't sleep or take much of a nap when he was sick. We were all desperate for sleep. Patrick was having more choking episodes and liquid build-up in his throat before getting sick. The cold made that worse. We'd been in contact with hospice and his doctor. I prayed that we would be able to keep him comfortable and that the cold would pass quickly and would not turn into pneumonia. I also prayed that we would figure out a way to help all of us get some sleep.

Our prayers were answered on July 15th. We all got some rest that night. Sleep was such a wonderful thing for all of us. I had slept with Patrick for most of that night. He was restless, but he awoke less irritable than he had been. We took it easy as he got better. While Patrick was resting in Steve's arms, I walked on the treadmill in our exercise room, which had a large, west-facing window. A beautiful Ponderosa pine tree stood just outside the window. I walked and listened to sad music on the iPod while a short-lived rainstorm passed over the Faded Rose, giving a much-needed drink to our parched grass. Raindrops on the front gate acted like prisms, creating tiny, luminous jewels that sparkled briefly and then disappeared. A robin enjoyed the ephemeral puddles in our driveway. After my exercise, I fed the horses and picked a small bouquet of flowers from the pasture. I thanked God for rest. I prayed that Patrick's cold would pass as quickly as the storm that had passed over us.

Soon but Not Right Now

Patrick and I started to have some serious conversations about heaven while he was sick. He'd been crying in his sleep and was very sad from time to time. When I asked him why he was sad, he told me that he was worried about us. He wanted to know that we (his mom and dad) would be okay. I shared what I had learned from reading, *Everlasting Life,* a book by David D. Swanson, given to us by Pastor Gary. I said, "Patrick, God loves you. It's okay. You can go to heaven when it is time. We will be fine. Our PEPC family will take care of us. We'll see you in heaven." Ginny, our hospice social worker, told me that I might need to tell him that many, many times.

The angel was with us every day. Patrick said he thought he was going to heaven soon, but not right now. He wanted to go to Cabela's first. And maybe Arizona, where his dear friend Jacob was spending the summer. He talked about how glad he was that Yetti, the horse he rode at Promise Ranch, had been here on Earth for him to ride and love. This may sound strange to some, but a Promise Ranch volunteer and I noticed that Yetti, who always lowered his head so Patrick could interact with him from his wheelchair, seemed almost sad when we said good-bye at the end of our riding session. Ginny and Dora, both from hospice, said that animals know things we can't explain.

I had been wondering if Patrick would go to heaven soon. He was still fighting the cold. I knew that illness could lower his seizure threshold. He struggled to breathe, and his face and liver had been hurting. His liver was slightly larger than it was at his last doctor's visit. I was still concerned about the possibility of pneumonia, which he had twice before this. Dora, our hospice nurse, checked his lungs, and they were clear. I thanked God for that.

Niemann-Pick had caused changes on the outside and the inside of his body. The low muscle tone we saw on the outside was also happening to him on the inside. His throat was not as open as it used to be. His nasal passages were awfully narrow. We had seen pictures of his nasal passages when he was being tested for sleep apnea the previous summer. It was no wonder that his face hurt. We were doing everything we could to keep him comfortable.

I read and reread "Everlasting Life." Swanson's words, explaining that God had a purpose and plan for our lives, comforted me. I prayed that we would lean on God and trust His will for our lives. I prayed that

Patrick would get over his cold quickly. I also prayed for protection so that Steve and I would not get sick. We barely had the energy to do what we needed to do day to day.

A Washing Machine of Grief

Things got more challenging the next week because Patrick and I were both ill. Patrick couldn't go to several of his therapies, and I didn't feel well enough to exercise. No endorphins for me. Steve had more doctor's appointments. I was concerned about him and hoping for answers. I talked to Ginny about grief. I had been thinking of grief in terms of waves. As a writer, I lived in metaphor land, so what she said really made sense to me. She compared grief to being in a washing machine. She said it was healthy to process feelings as they welled up within each of us when we thought about Patrick going to heaven before we did.

Every August for several years, I had participated in the women's sprint distance Tri for the Cure triathlon, always walking the running portion. In the past, Patrick had trained with me. He was my coach. We rode our bicycles and swam together. He and Steve always met me at the finish line. I wanted to do it again that summer, even though my training was minimal. The beginning of a triathlon in the lake has been compared to a washing machine, with the arms, legs, and feet of fifty or more people in a start wave thrashing in the water. I had experienced that sensation each year. It was truly like being in the agitate cycle. Another woman swam over me one year. *That* was a strange feeling. I had learned to protect my face while swimming, so I didn't get kicked in the eye. I was learning that I had to care for myself as we walked the NPC journey, so that grief didn't kick me in the eye, either. I was reaching out to others and asking for help, when I felt like I was being tossed about inside the washing machine of grief. I prayed for us to take each day one step at a time, asking for help as we needed it.

The Hands and Feet of Jesus

"Be strong and courageous. Do not be afraid or terrified because of them, for the LORD your God goes with you; *he will never leave you nor forsake you.*" (Dt 31:6)

God sent me a strong message on July 23rd. I saw the hands and feet of Jesus at work. Many volunteers from the Helping Hands Community Outreach Project and PEPC's Handyman Ministry helped with phase one of the deck project at the Faded Rose Ranch—demolition. Both the front and back decks had been falling apart. We were so blessed. Work would be completed in August. God certainly knew me better than I knew myself. He knew that we felt like we were all alone on the NPC journey with Patrick. That day God showed me, a bull-headed Norwegian, again, without a doubt, that we *were not* alone, and that He would never leave us nor forsake us. Sometimes I needed a lightning bolt or a large group of people showing up at my house to get my attention. It worked. God knew me so well.

Unfortunately, Patrick had another one of his violent episodes at noon that day. It took both of us to hold him down and keep him safe. We came close to calling 911 for help. Afterward, he was okay. We were okay. We had not had one of those episodes since February. It may have been brought on by all the excitement and the changes to the decks. He was frustrated that he couldn't walk through the doors where the decks had been. He didn't understand that there was now a drop-off to the ground. We could only exit through the garage door until the decks were rebuilt. We asked for a hospice nurse to come out to visit. We prayed that we would get his dosages adjusted, so that we could keep him at home with us. We didn't want to hospitalize him.

A Bride Coming Down from Heaven

> I saw the Holy City, the new Jerusalem, coming down out of heaven from God, prepared as a bride beautifully dressed for her husband. And I heard a loud voice from the throne saying, 'Look! God's dwelling place is now among the people, and he will dwell with them. They will be his people, and God himself will be with them and be their God. He will wipe every tear from their eyes. There will be no more death or mourning or crying or pain, for the old order of things has passed away.' (Rv 21: 2–4)

We made some changes to Patrick's prescriptions and were seeing more of the old Patrick. He was less tired and more animated. It was so nice to see his smile and to hear him laugh. We read the Bible with Patrick every day. I didn't always know if he was paying attention. We had been reading a lot in Revelation. When Patrick talked about the new deck that we would be blessed with in August, he said, "It will be like a bride coming down from heaven." *He had been listening.* I praised the Lord when I heard that. We were so thankful that a group of volunteers would come to our home to rebuild the decks and help with repairs. It is an incredible blessing from God.

Waste Not, Want Not

I helped Patrick shuffle to the barn to visit Shakira, before she went to heaven on July 29th. Our good-byes were bittersweet. We were happy that she would no longer be in pain, but we would miss her.

"What do horses and mules *do* in heaven?" Patrick asked.

"Run free," I said. That seemed to give him peace. I didn't realize at the time that my wishful thinking was not based upon biblical teaching. We talked a lot about who would be waiting in heaven for Shakira and for him, when it was time. He knew he would learn the answers to all his questions when he met the Lord.

While we were in the barn, I showed Patrick the barn swallows and their mud nests on the metal ceiling. We thought we saw a little bird peeking out at us from one of the nests. The barn smelled sweet. Two of the four stalls were full—piled floor to ceiling with year-old hay that had been donated to DHOH. "Waste not, want not," was what I had learned growing up. Freshly opened wood shavings spread on the ground in the stalls added to the perfume.

We had a wonderful visit that afternoon with Grace, a friend of Patrick's, who was now in college. She had met Patrick in ninth grade, when she had helped in the special education room at Legend High School. It was good for Patrick to see someone else near his age facing her own health challenges with such a positive attitude. Grace filled our home with a happy light.

We read in Psalms together that night as a family as Pastor Doug at PEPC suggested. We were learning that God really did want to know our hearts—the good, the bad, and even the ugly. I prayed that we would walk closer to God every day.

Chapter Nine

August

Please Smile at Him

At the end of May, I had wondered if Patrick would able to return to Legend High School. In early August, we decided that Patrick would be going to school once a week, on Mondays. Praise God! The plan was to visit the special education room and then go to ceramics, his favorite class, with an aide. We would be there less than an hour. I was praying that it would be a positive experience for him. The kids in his special needs cohort loved him and were always happy to see him, but in his junior year, I had noticed that most of the neurotypical kids, in the ceramics room, avoided eye contact and did not talk with him. It broke my heart.

He never said anything, but I think that on some level he noticed. After talking with another parent whose child had obvious medical challenges and attended school, I followed her suggestion that we talk with Patrick's class and encourage them to ask questions about his disease. I prayed that kids would smile at him and talk with him. There was only limited response from the students.

We had a new rescue horse, Fuzzy. She was learning to trust me. I was frustrated because Fuzzy resisted my efforts to give her food and attention. While trying to get her to come to eat one afternoon, I wondered if God ever got frustrated with us. He has so much love to give us, if we would only trust Him.

We watched the movie, *90 Minutes in Heaven* together. Pastor Gary had given us three helpful books: *90 Minutes in Heaven, Heaven Is Real,* and *Everlasting Life.* We had been sharing information from the books with Patrick. When I found the movie based upon the book, I knew we had to have it. After watching it, Patrick said emphatically, "I can't wait to get to heaven!" I prayed that we would learn to trust God fully as we walked our NPC journey.

I See You, Patrick

Patrick hit a rough patch in early August. It was so hard to be a sixteen-year-old young man living in what was rapidly becoming an old man's body. His care was becoming more involved. We were working to get respite and additional nursing support in place.

A dear friend of ours wrote a beautiful poem, "I See You," about Patrick. Lisa, the author, had known our family since Patrick was a little boy. When she came to visit us, she said that she could still see the Patrick she knew in his eyes.

I See You, Patrick

I see you, Patrick
Through your bright blue eyes,
That little boy running under bright blue skies.

I see you, Patrick,
Little boy with dreams
The police man, the builder, the boyish schemes.

I see you, Patrick,
Young man growing up;
Caring, compassion, you never give up.

I see you, Patrick,
A young man on the go,
Serving others, you're a privilege to know.

I see you, Patrick,
As your body gives way,
Your faith grows stronger, stronger each day.

I see you, Patrick,
Though others may not.
Who you are, will not be forgot.

I see you, Patrick,
Through a shell giving way,
You are becoming more like Jesus with each
passing day.

continued

I see you, Patrick,
As your Spirit prepares for its permanent home,
Jesus is with you; you won't be alone,

I see you, Patrick,
Shining His light,
Teaching us all, it's going to be all right,

I see you, Patrick,
Full of joy and peace,
In the arms of the Father, finally complete.

—Lisa J. Barila[5]

Following Patrick's Lead

After watching the storms on radar all summer, we had figured out that the Faded Rose sat just north of where storms tracked in our area. We could also tell this by looking at the mature trees' growth patterns. Things were dusty and dry, but there were still some tiny yellow and purple flowers in the pasture. Steve, with assistance from the Handyman Ministry at PEPC, got the sprinkler system working. Trees that had looked nearly dead were starting to show growth.

The Faded Rose would soon be filled with volunteers, working to replace the decks, completing much-needed repairs, and doing yard work. We were so blessed. We praised God for his steadfast love and provision for us. Pastor Gary told us that this was an opportunity for us to learn humility, a hard but necessary lesson for us.

It helped to know we were not alone as we watched Patrick's slow decline. I was learning to listen to and watch for Patrick's subtle changes. For example, he no longer wanted to ride Yetti at Promise Ranch. It made sense if I paid attention because we had gradually transitioned from riding an hour with little assistance three years ago, down to fifteen minutes and several volunteers, with Patrick being exhausted at the brief lesson's end. Thankfully, the teachers had been wonderful in coming up with ways for Patrick to interact with Yetti and the other critters at Promise Ranch.

I continued to pray for safety and the ability to meet Patrick's needs as they arose.

Amen and Praise the Lord

"Praise the Lord, my soul; all my inmost being, praise His holy name. Praise the Lord, my soul, and forget not all his benefits" (Ps 103:1–2).

Patrick and I watched a forklift carry deck materials from a large truck on County Road 13 to our driveway while we loaded the wheelchair van one morning. As I talked with Doil Storie from Helping Hands, who was supervising the delivery, I heard Patrick's voice in the van shouting, "Amen and praise the Lord!" Patrick was *so excited* to have new decks! He loved to eat outside and watch the DHOH rescue horses, Fancy Pants, Serendipity, and Fuzzy Wuzzy grazing in the pasture that wrapped all the way around our little house. We also enjoyed watching the hummingbirds visit the red feeder we had hung in the large, old Ponderosa pine tree that shaded the back of our home. Steve used a secret nectar recipe that the hummingbirds really loved. The wind in the tree had such a sweet, calming sound.

Our old front and back decks had been falling apart and had nails sticking out through the peeling paint. The new decks built by Helping Hands would never need painting and would be accessible to Patrick from inside the house. It would be like adding two new rooms to the house. The new, large deck on the east side would allow us to sit outside and look for beautiful sunrises, moonrises, and rainbows. A new front porch deck on the west side would have a small bench near the door, and we would be able to see all the way to Pike's Peak.

Volunteers who visited the Faded Rose were greeted by happy wild sunflowers growing near the mailbox. When I thought about the amazing blessings we were receiving from the volunteers, I started crying. I had been crying *a lot* of happy tears since preparations had begun. I sang these words from the Doxology we used to sing in church when I was a little girl, "Praise God from whom all blessings flow!"

Our joy was overflowing. We were rocking out to *You Shake the Earth* by Central Live in the van while on our way to adaptive swimming. We so appreciated that Kristen Cotter had shared such wonderful Christian music with us. I'm sure people in other cars wondered why we were singing so loudly. It was our new favorite. I loved the part about a hurricane of grace in that song.

Patrick had some episodes when his heart rate got so high that it scared him. He refused to use oxygen. We also continued to adjust Patrick's medication to help with his aggression. We prayed for wisdom as we did that. We wanted to hang on to Patrick's fun personality for as long as we could *and* keep all of us safe.

Let's Dine Al Fresco!

"Let's dine al fresco," Patrick said joyously early on the Sunday morning after the decks were completed. He had learned that phrase from his dad, Steve, who used to say it a lot while Patrick was young. Patrick was excited to eat a sunrise breakfast on the deck, even though there was a cold wind blowing at the time. We all bundled up in our robes and huddled at a table on the beautiful back deck built with loving hands by the volunteers at our home. We were *so thankful* for all the hard work done by the caring workers.

The Faded Rose looked like a different place. Volunteers had replaced rotting wood trim and painted around the windows, giving the house a totally different look. The water damage along our home's base had been completely repaired. Brave volunteers fought off wasps and spiders while trimming bushes and trees and while repairing and painting a fence around the yard's perimeter.

I particularly appreciated that we didn't feel any judgment from the volunteers. It was hard for us to accept their help. Learning humility had been a huge lesson for all of us. One volunteer called their work a "God Hug," and it did indeed feel like God was wrapping loving arms around our family. Patrick loved watching the workers use power tools to help build the deck. Helping Hands was even going to make a video about the completed project.

It was certainly a weekend of miracles. Volunteers from Professionals Miracles Foundation, who happened to be helping on the Helping Hands crew, stopped working to present a check to our family. One of our sweet friends, Susan Meyer, had applied for a grant on our behalf. We were grateful for her efforts. The money would help so much since I had stopped working as an elementary classroom teacher, so I could care for Patrick. Professionals Miracles Foundation helped families who were in situations like ours. We hadn't even known they existed.

I kept singing, "Praise God from whom all blessings flow."

In the Shelter of Your Wings

Hear my cry, O God; listen to my prayer. From the ends of the earth I call to you, I call as my heart grows faint; lead me to the rock that is higher than I. For you have been my refuge, a strong tower against the foe. I long to dwell in your tent forever and take refuge in the shelter of your wings. (Ps 61:1–4)

The middle of August was a rollercoaster of emotions for me. I went from singing praises to crying, what felt like a thousand tears. Some days were unbelievably difficult. We were having difficulty keeping up with medication changes needed to keep us all safe. I couldn't imagine how Patrick felt inside, when he was so out of control. I held him during his two-hour naps, and Steve held him long after he fell asleep, so Patrick would feel safe and loved. Our faith in God was what sustained us. We prayed for safety and for peace in our hearts and in our home.

A Wilderness of My Own Making

The Israelites had moved about in the wilderness forty years until all the men who were of military age when they left Egypt had died, since they had not obeyed the Lord. For the Lord had sworn to them that they would not see the land he had solemnly promised their ancestors to give us, a land flowing with milk and honey. (Jo 5:6)

On August 16th, two people who worked with Patrick noticed that his eyes and demeanor were unusual. It was like he was a different person. The next day, Patrick got mad at God for his NPC and what it was doing to him. He flashed to frustration and rage so quickly. We talked about it, and I urged him, as others had done, to ask God to help him as he went through difficult times.

I thanked God for Patrick's childlike faith in Him and in heaven because his faith had made me think about my own faith in a new way. Patrick's decision to accept Christ had led us to our church home at PEPC. I had come to a point where I could honestly thank God for NPC because it had brought me to my knees—literally. I had to pray all day long just to keep going from moment to moment.

Steve and I were preparing to reaffirm our faith. We had been baptized as infants, but we were choosing to take this next step to reaffirm our faith together by returning to our baptismal waters. I was amazed every day at the work the Lord was doing in my husband. I loved the man he was becoming. For me, this reaffirmation of faith was an opportunity to begin again and do it right. I was glad that God pursued me for forty years, while I was in a wilderness of my own making. I discovered the song, "Pursue Me" by Worship Central as we counted down to our special day.

Racers, Start Your Engines

> "I restore the crushed spirit of the humble and revive the courage of those with repentant hearts" (Is 57:15 NLT).

> In the same way the Spirit helps us in our weakness. We do not know what we ought to pray for, but the Spirit himself intercedes for us through wordless groans. (Rom 8:26)

Patrick started to breathe hard when he was just sitting still or lying down. He didn't like it when I used the fingertip pulse oximeter, but when he allowed me to slip it on his finger without trying to destroy it, I watched his heart rate rev up to the 140s from his resting heart rate of about 120. Our wonderful hospice nurse, Dora, said the racing would continue to happen and that it might go up to 170 or more.

We had more serious choking episodes. After one incident, he had to lie down to rest. He loved to eat, and sometimes he ate so much, that he threw up. We gently reminded him to limit his portions. His eyes were truly bigger than his stomach. Hospice told us to let him eat what he liked. He'd always been an oral kid, and eating was one thing that still brought him joy. We didn't want to take that away from him.

"Jesus, I'm talking to you," Patrick said confidently, one night as he was falling asleep. We had been working with him to say short prayers for help when he feels himself getting angry. Patrick had heard me say, "Lord, help me," since he was a baby. We had also learned a quick, three-word prayer, "Jesus, help me!" from Pastor Gary. Sometimes all he had a chance to cry out was, "Jesus!" We believed that God was able to understand Patrick's unspoken plea for help. One of our favorite songs was, "Cry Out to Jesus" by Third Day. We didn't know that just one month later we would be listening to that song as Patrick lay in my arms in the hospice care center.

Lessons in Love

> See what great love the Father has lavished on us, that we should be called children of God! And that is what we are! The reason the world does not know us is that it did not know him. (1 Jn 3:1)

> For as high as the heavens are above the earth, so great is his love for those who fear him; as far as the east is from the west, so far has he removed our transgressions from us. As a father has compassion on his children, so the Lord has compassion on those who fear him. (Ps 103: 11–13)

'For I know the plans I have for you,' declares the Lord, 'plans to prosper you and not to harm you, plans to give you hope and a future.' (Jer 29:11)

Fuzzy Wuzzy, one of our rescues, would not eat softened grain from me when she first arrived, even though her ribs were showing. I got frustrated with her, and I wondered if God ever got frustrated with me when I did not trust in Him. Fuzzy couldn't have known that the Faded Rose Ranch was a safe place and that I only wanted to lavish love upon her and find her a loving, forever home. I had learned a great deal from Fuzzy; the most important lesson being that love is based upon trust. Fuzzy was learning to take food from me, Patrick, and others who volunteered at the Faded Rose. I loved to hear her soft nicker when she saw me walking toward the barn. She was starting to allow me to touch her and groom her, but I still couldn't put a halter on her.

Steve and I were also slowly learning to trust others. People who we should have been able to trust in our past had cruelly betrayed us. Pastor Gary and our PEPC family faithfully continued to reach out and care for us, and we were learning that not everyone had an agenda or an ulterior motive behind their actions. We had come so far from the isolated, lonely island of distrust on which we had been living.

August 23rd was one of those days that I wondered if it would be our last day together. For part of the day, Patrick seemed so far away from us. We were not sure if it was medication or disease progression or a combination of both, but it was becoming harder and harder for Patrick to communicate. However, he was able to joyfully say, "I am so glad that you and Dad are reaffirming your faith!" Looking back, I am so glad that we had many heartfelt conversations about heaven, Jesus, and faith in God. I didn't know that Patrick would be taking Jesus's hand in just one month. I prayed for us to have strength because I was feeling overwhelmed by sadness and fear.

A Step of Faith

Patrick saw us reaffirm our faith at Aurora Reservoir, one of our favorite places in the world. We had sailed and ridden our bikes there for years as a family. He was *so excited.* We had a plan in place in case he suddenly decided to join us in the water. Thankfully he watched quietly from the shore. We were incredibly thankful that Pastor Gary had gently and patiently guided us to that step of faith. Our sweet friends helped keep Patrick happy, safe, and occupied during the service and lunch. That was quite a challenge because he was unsteady on his feet but sometimes still wanted to get up and go without asking for help.

It was hard to put into words just how we were feeling that day. Patrick saw us take a giant step in our faith together, and it reassured him that we knew the Lord, loved the Lord, and wanted to follow His plan for our lives. Most importantly, I think it gave him confidence that we would walk *with* the Lord until we were *all* together in heaven one day. He saw how our PEPC family loved and supported us. He didn't articulate it, but I think it gave him a deep sense of peace and answered his concerns about our being okay after he went home to heaven. I loved the words about baptism and living for the first time that I found in a song by Third Day, called "Born Again."

We each chose a verse to share at the service. Steve's verse was the same one Pastor Gary had given us at the outset of our NPC journey—the scripture that I still carried on a well-worn card in my pocket. "Do not be anxious about anything, but in every situation, by prayer and petition, with thanksgiving, present your requests to God. And the peace of God, which transcends all understanding, will guard your hearts and your minds in Christ Jesus" (Phil 4:6–7).

My special verse reflected the painful, but life-changing lesson I had learned from walking our NPC journey. "And we know that in all things God works for the good of those who love him, who have been called according to his purpose." (Rom 8:28). God had brought me to the end of myself so that I could hear His "still small voice" calling to me (1 Kgs 19:12 KJV). I was learning to trust God's plan for our lives.

And Then a Pretty Girl Walked By

At the end of August, NPC was rapidly changing Patrick and was making things dangerous at times. I don't use the word *hate* easily, but I hated what the disease was doing to Patrick. I hated how unsafe things were. I hated the choices we were having to make about his care. We met with the hospice team to ask for additional nursing support at home. We prayed for clarity about how to keep Patrick and our family safe. We also prayed to feel God's peace again.

While driving in the wheelchair van, Patrick and I had a serious discussion comparing living on Earth to living in heaven because there had been times recently when he had begged us to let him go to heaven. He was about to explain which was better: heaven or Earth, when a carload of pretty high school girls pulled up next to us. *Of course,* he said *Earth was better.* He *was* a teenage boy, after all.

Chapter Ten

September

I Can Do All This

"I can do all this through Him who gives me strength" (Phil 4:13).

In early September, Patrick started a low dose of a new medication to help manage his aggression. It made him groggy and wobbly. Sadly, he was still aggressive, especially toward his dad, Steve, and sometimes toward me. His speech was almost unintelligible at times. We continued to adjust his medications. Thankfully, his sense of humor emerged from time to time. I prayed each day that we would not lose that part of him to his disease.

Several small challenges happened. First, I sprained my ankle. (Sprained and/or broken ankles have become an annual event for me.) Friends offered to help. One dear friend met me at urgent care and even loaned me a boot so that I would not have to buy one. The horses were curious about the plastic bag I wore over the boot when I went out to the pasture.

Then, we had several flat tires. A visiting nurse even had a flat. One Sunday morning, we discovered a low tire on the way to church. Thankfully, we were able get home and switch cars before it went all the way flat. That was no easy task with loading and unloading the wheelchair. We were late to church, but we made it. We think the demolition project had left behind nails. We decided to buy a magnetic broom to sweep the driveway and hopefully prevent future flats.

Finally, a barn clean-up project I had started turned into a several-day effort to clean out many inches of dirt, old signs, carpeting, and shingles. Steve and our friends helped with the work. We were so blessed to have such caring friends. We prayed that we would trust in God to give us the strength we needed to face each challenge as it arose.

Prayers, Please

> For this very reason, make every effort to supplement your faith with virtue, and virtue with knowledge, and knowledge with self-control, and self-control with steadfastness, and steadfastness with godliness, and godliness with brotherly affection, and brotherly affection with love. (2 Pt 1:5–7 ESV)

I was brutally honest in my September 6 journal entry. It was one of our hardest days, partly because it started at 2 a.m. I didn't do well on two hours of sleep. It was becoming harder and harder for Patrick to express himself. I had been able to align my thinking with his and finish his thought or figure out what he was trying to say. Now his thoughts didn't make sense to me. He repeated things over and over and over—sometimes up to seven times. He also seemed disconnected from his body, so it was difficult for him to ask for what he needed physically. He went straight to frustration and rage. We continued to work with the hospice team to adjust Patrick's meds.

Steve was able to take extended time off from his work. We were hoping that respite care might start soon. Patrick had met his new caregiver and enjoyed spending time with her. We would be close at hand, and another caregiver would give us much-needed help with Patrick's increasing needs.

I asked friends and family to continue to lift us up in prayer. I prayed that Steve and I would have infinite patience and the ability to look beyond being cursed at, flipped off, hit, and kicked. I also prayed that we would be able to step back and be able to figure out what Patrick needed, but could not ask for in each moment. I prayed for our physical and emotional health. I also prayed for our marriage. The stress of caring for Patrick was tearing at the fabric of our relationship. I prayed that we would lean on God together.

Crickets, Coyotes, and the Fine Art of Flinging Manure

> He speaks to the sun and it does not shine; he seals off the light of the stars. He alone stretches out the heavens and treads on the waves of the sea. He is the Maker of the Bear and Orion, the Pleiades and the constellations of the south. (Jb 9:7–9)

The next week brought many changes. Patrick's new medication made him groggy and unsteady. He was sedated throughout the day. We were monitoring him closely, because we were concerned that he might be having an allergic reaction to the drugs. He was somewhat less aggressive but had started to spit up his medicine and food more and more. Patrick's breathing often seemed ragged when he was sleeping. He had strange dreams that frightened him. I held him at night to help him fall back to sleep after each dream. One warm evening that week, we had all the windows open after the sun went down. The coyotes, who usually seemed far away, were howling all around us. It was an eerie sound—disturbing.

I went outside early the next morning to feed the horses. The stars were boldly beautiful. Orion seemed to be hunting right over our barn. Crickets were chirping, and someone's rooster wanted to get an early start on the day. The last roses were saying goodbye to summer at the Faded Rose. Purple asters, one of my favorite flowers, carpeted the yard.

A wonderful group of young men volunteered to clean up the pasture over the weekend. We used the manure spreader, and I also taught them the fine art of flinging horse poop. Step one: Check wind direction. Do not throw manure into the wind. Step two: Throw sideways, not over your head.

Steve and I were learning to take care of ourselves, so that we would have something left to give to Patrick. We so appreciated the help that others gave us that week. We prayed that we could keep Patrick safe when moving him within the house. We were also praying that we would get trained medical assistance as we needed it.

May I Have This Dance?

"I am torn between the two: I desire to depart and be with Christ, which is better by far" (Phil 1:23).

We started using a shuffle transition that we learned from hospice. Patrick put his arms around my neck, and we stood close together and shuffled from his wheelchair to the bed or from his wheelchair to the couch. We called it our dance. It was working, but it was challenging, because Patrick was several inches taller than I was and about forty pounds heavier. I was still wearing an ankle support. We prayed all day that we could keep him safe. He wanted to get up and move around, and he didn't understand that he was sedated. We had figured out that we could feed him during the times that he was a little more awake, he was able to swallow safely, but we still had lots of choking and coughing. He was barely able to speak. We were all incredibly sad. Lots of tears. He *adamantly* did not want a feeding tube or a breathing tube. He wanted to go to heaven. It was painfully hard. We prayed for safety and additional support.

He's Getting My Room Ready

My Father's house has many rooms; if that were not so, would I have told you that I am going there to prepare a place for you? And if

I go and prepare a place for you, I will come back and take you to be with me that you also may be where I am. (Jn 14: 2–3)

On September 14th, about six o'clock in the morning, Patrick said haltingly, "Jesus...*the real one*...is here."

"In this room?" I asked.

"*Yes,*" he whispered.

A little while later, I asked Patrick if Jesus was still with us.

"No. *He's in heaven...he's getting my room ready,*" Patrick said.

It was exactly ten days before Patrick would go home to be with the Lord.

Nurses from Denver Hospice had told us that kids would talk about seeing angels or Jesus as they prepared to die and go to heaven. I was so glad that we could still talk with Patrick during the times when the medicine had worn off a bit. We were getting better at transfers. I asked friends to continue to pray for safety and sleep for all of us. Their prayers brought us comfort and peace.

Counting Our Blessings

"Rejoice always, pray continually, give thanks in all circumstances; for this is God's will for you in Christ Jesus" (1 Thes 5:16–18).

Patrick started using the lift at the therapy pool in mid-September. His wonderful teacher, Terry Harkins Bickel, knew exactly what to say. She told Patrick the lift was a roller coaster ride. He loved it. Patrick had always been a water baby, swimming and sailing since *before* he was born. We loved going to the pool. It brought us joy, but my heart was breaking as I pushed the button to lower Patrick into the water. I pasted a happy smile on my face, so I wouldn't spoil the moment for him. It was one more loss. Terry later told me that she saw a weariness in Patrick's eyes that day that she had not seen before.

I was trying to focus on our blessings, but it was hard. The lift was a blessing because it allowed us to continue going to the pool three times a week. The rec center had large family dressing rooms we could use, which was a blessing. The therapy pool was a warm ninety degrees, so Patrick wouldn't get the shakes from getting cold. That was a blessing. Terry had the knowledge, experience, tools, and creative ideas to make Patrick's time in the water safe and fun, definitely another blessing. Terry kept Patrick's face out of the water since he was so sleepy. He was safe and happy in the water that he loved—a blessing. While they worked together, I swam laps in the regular pool, which was just steps away from them. The mental and physical break was a blessing for me. Terry went above and beyond and always pushed the wheelchair to the deck shower and the sauna after his lesson to give me a break. So many blessings. I prayed that we would focus on our blessings and not on our losses.

Not My Will but Thine—Going into the Hospice Care Center

On Saturday, September 17th, we noticed a significant change in Patrick. He was unusually tired and kept falling to his left. We thought his meds were possibly causing the changes. I took him to visit Yetti, his horse at equine therapy, that morning. His therapist had put carrots and finger-paint on a large poster. Patrick smiled a giant smile while his therapy horse, Yetti, *painted* a colorful picture while chasing the carrots with his nose.

When we got home, Patrick collapsed on his bed instead of going to the couch to watch his favorite television shows. I called hospice, thinking we needed to make a medication change. A nurse came out, checked on Patrick, and suggested that we take him to the hospice care center for further evaluation. As the ambulance drivers rolled him on a gurney out of our house, a part of me wondered if Patrick would ever come home again. I rode with him in the back of the ambulance. Steve followed behind us. They didn't run lights or sirens but monitored him closely on the long ride into the city.

We arrived at the hospice care center late in the afternoon. The wonderful hospice center chef prepared scrambled eggs and bacon for Patrick because he *loved* bacon. That same chef came to visit Patrick and brought a bacon cheeseburger for him just a couple of days later, on his day off. Sadly, by that time Patrick had stopped eating. I broke off a piece of bacon and put it in his mouth for him to taste it, gently removing it when he didn't chew or swallow. The last food he tasted was his favorite food—bacon.

The nurses at hospice encouraged us to leave the room from time to time, but we only wanted to stay with Patrick and hold him. They found a bed that was big enough for all three of us to squeeze into together. We had wanted Patrick to die at home in our arms, but it quickly became apparent that Patrick wasn't going back to the Faded Rose Ranch.

Five Hundred and Fifty Days Later

As the deer pants for streams of water, so my soul pants for you, my God. My soul thirsts for God, for the living God. When can I go and meet with God? (Ps 42:1–2)

Five hundred and fifty days after our first divine appointment with Pastor Gary, we met with him again, this time in a shadowed hospice room, joined by Patrick's father, talking, praying, and quietly singing "Ten Thousand Reasons." I held Patrick in a hospital bed as his life on this Earth was slipping away. Patrick was declining rapidly. He had stopped eating and drinking. His resting pulse rate and temperature were climbing. The words we sang about one's strength failing at the end of this earthly life were particularly poignant. It was almost time for Patrick to go home to be with Jesus. We asked others to pray for us to feel God's peace and strength and for Patrick to have a peaceful transition to heaven.

Two Chaplains, a Rabbi, and a Pastor Walked into a Room

"Jesus answered, 'I am the way and the truth and the life. No one comes to the Father except through me'" (Jn 14:6).

Patrick's hospice room was filled with tears, prayers, stories, singing, and yes, even laughter. Even though Patrick had stopped talking and his eyes were closed, hospice nurses told us he could hear everything going on around him. I think he approved of the laughter, *because he had always loved to laugh.* Pastor Gary stopped by to talk, sing, and pray with us. Shortly after he left, I kid you not, two chaplains and a rabbi walked into the room. The chaplains attended PEPC and the rabbi was from Denver Hospice. It provided a moment of comic relief for all of us.

So many wonderful visitors, both human and animal, including service dogs who licked Patrick's hand, came to say goodbye to Patrick. There was even some talk of a secret mission, complete with diversionary tactics, to sneak a pony into his room for a visit.

A special friend came to visit Patrick. Before Patrick stopped talking, he had told me that he really wanted to see this friend before he died. We shared the story of Patrick's faith with them and how Patrick was hoping that all his friends would have relationships with Jesus so that he could be with them in heaven one day.

We were grateful for everyone who brought food and drinks during our week-long stay at the hospice care center. We appreciated the friends who sat next to Patrick, so that we could get rest. His room was filled with artwork, flowers, gifts, and so much love. We were truly blessed.

Patrick Fought the Good Fight and He Finished the Race

Patrick Chandler Zimmermann went home to be with his heavenly Father late on a Saturday evening. Patrick spent the last week of his life at the Denver Hospice Care Center. He had such a big, strong heart—so full of love. His heart rate soared to 180 in the hours before he died. The three of us snuggled in an oversized hospital bed together. We prayed, read scripture, sang songs, told stories, and held Patrick in our arms. He stirred and reached out as he was passing. We could sense Jesus was in the room with us, taking Patrick's hand and leading him home.

We told friends that Patrick wanted his memorial service to be a celebration. He had requested that people wear bright colors, camo, or Western wear. We also asked people to write down special memories that they had of Patrick or to describe how his life and faith impacted their life, and share that with us. Those memories would help us get through the hard days ahead without him.

Chapter Eleven

Finding Meaning in the Dark Days

> However many years anyone may live, let them enjoy them all. But let them remember the days of darkness, for there will be many. Everything to come is meaningless. (Eccl 11:8)

Shockingly Silent

> He will wipe every tear from their eyes. There will be no more death or mourning or crying or pain, for the old order of things has passed away. (Rv 21:4)

We said goodbye to Patrick's earth-suit that week. He was dressed from head to toe in camouflage. Nearly everything he wore was given to him by a caring friend. His camo shirt was emblazoned with a Broncos logo. Even his socks were camo. He wore a handmade friendship bracelet painstakingly cut from a baseball. His cargo pockets were filled with treasures. He carried a cross, his baptismal Bible verse, stickers for his heavenly longboard, a Broncos lanyard, a baseball for heavenly baseball games, and the tissues we had used to wipe away our tears after he died peacefully in our arms. I knew there would be no tears in heaven, but there had been many tears cried here on Earth. The Faded Rose Ranch was shockingly silent without him.

We had 6,070 treasured days with Patrick. I prayed for the strength to walk into the sanctuary for Patrick's memorial service. I asked God to give us the ability to put one foot in front of the other as we made that long walk down to the front pew in church and in the days to come.

A Filly Called Hopeful

"The Lord is close to the brokenhearted and saves those who are crushed in spirit" (Ps 34:18).

God gave us something to focus on after Patrick died. A rescue mare and her filly, named Hopeful, came to stay with us. They and another horse had been rescued from Louisiana after historic flooding. Sick, starved, and near death, I had to give Hopeful medicine in her grain twice a day. Hopeful was a smart, feisty little thing—a real spitfire—just what I needed to help me have a reason to get out of bed each day. Caring for Hopeful and her momma started us on the road to healing. We all got stronger together. After a time, Steve returned to work, and I found a part-time teaching position. Pastor Gary met with us several times. He also gave us booklets every few months about how to survive the first year after a loss. At his urging, we took a GriefShare class together and tried to make sense of our life without Patrick. The faith-based class taught us to "just do the next thing" when we felt paralyzed by our grief. Believing Patrick was with Jesus helped us put one foot in front of the other. We grieved in different ways and at different times, but we buoyed one another when waves of grief crashed over us.[6]

Our phones fell silent as people gave us space to grieve. Those who had lost a child leaned in. Others fell away. I think they weren't sure what to say. "I'm so very sorry for your loss," is the perfect thing to say. So is sharing stories about the person who died and asking to look at picture albums together. One sweet family came out every week. Their son, Mathew, a friend of Patrick's since their soccer days, became our ranch hand, helping us care for the rescue horses.

We leaned on our church family and spent more and more time reading the Word. Someone nominated us to be deacons so that we would have a way to serve together. I started to serve on the vocal worship team. I felt closer to Patrick when I sang in church, as if the veil between heaven and earth was thin. I could visualize him singing and praising God right beside me. Praying and writing poetry helped me process my tangled ball of feelings. Patrick had been our whole world. Steve and I talked to God all the time.

I asked Him to help us build a life that had meaning. About a month after Patrick died, I heard that PEPC's high school youth group was having an informational meeting about their annual summer mission trip to an orphanage in Fond Blanc, Haiti. They needed adults to help supervise the students from PEPC. I felt God urging me to sign up. He called. I answered. I watched the video of the previous year's trip over and over. The orphans' sweet faces tugged at my heartstrings. Planning and saving for the trip gave me something to work toward, something on which to focus.

While preparing for the trip, Spencer, one of Patrick's friends, told me about Steve, a young handicapped boy with a rickety wheelchair whom she had met the previous summer during PEPC's mission trip. Steve lived in Cazale, a village not too far from the orphanage. One thing led to another, and we decided to take Patrick's wheelchair to him. We communicated with Steve's family through the Fond Blanc Foundation that sponsors the orphanage. We learned that Steve's wheelchair completely fell apart just one week before we arrived in Haiti. He and his parents were overjoyed to receive the wheelchair. I learned a little Haitian Creole and shared Patrick's story with them through an interpreter. I was able to spend several memorable hours reading and singing to Steve while I was in Haiti.

Life slowly started to make sense. Steve and I felt that we were being led to serve God by walking alongside hurting families and sharing Patrick's story of faith. We understood the pain of losing a child, and we could share our story of God's faithfulness with others. "(God) who comforts us in all our troubles, so that we can comfort those in any trouble with the comfort we ourselves receive from God," (2 Cor 1:4).

The Place I Go to Remember

I touch my hand
to the cold, black stone,
and I remember.
I touch my fingers
to the dry soil at my feet
sprinkled with pine needles,
and I remember.
I watch the sun
slowly sinking in the winter sky,
and I remember.
I listen to the water flowing
in the water feature nearby,
and I remember.
A woman pushes a child in a baby stroller
past the Memorial Garden.
Cars rush by,
and a plane flies overhead,
but still I remember.
The wind whispers,
"Night is coming,
it's time to go,"
and the sky grows dark,
but still I remember.
My tears come
like a sudden storm,
and swiftly they are gone
Because I know
you are not here.
This is just the place I go
to remember.

—C. K. Zimmermann

God, I Don't Understand

I was talking with God in church yesterday,
everyone around me singing joyfully.
A part of me was joyful too, but another part
of my heart
was wrestling with God.
"God," I prayed, "I don't understand
why you gave me a heart
so full of love
and yet you only gave me
one son.
And then you took Patrick away from us
after only 6,070 days.
What do I do with all the love
left in my heart?"
Tenderly, His answer came.
"Love others as I have loved you.
Hold the baby
for the weary mother.
Take the hand
of one who is alone and lonely.
Walk beside someone who is seeking Me."
I am learning
a most painful lesson
that joy and pain must coexist in my heart
until we are together with Patrick again
in heaven.

—C. K. Zimmermann

Am I Still A Mother?

Mother's Day is fast approaching.
The first one without Patrick.
Am I still a mother, I ask myself?
My son is in heaven with Jesus.
Can I still celebrate
the precious gift God gave me?
How do I celebrate?
What do I celebrate?
Why would I want
to celebrate?
"God," I whispered,
"Help me out here.
My heart is hurting
and I don't know what to do
or what to say."
Just the other day,
a woman working at the bank
saw my Legend High School shirt
and asked when my son graduated.
"My son graduated to heaven,"
I told her.
She was taken aback.
I didn't mean to shock her.
But I'm still a mother.
I know you are safe with Jesus
until we are together again.

—C. K. Zimmermann

Because

Surrounded by families
full and complete.
Smiling, laughing,
bowing their heads to pray.
I feel a hole in my heart, Lord.
Because
the one I love
is with You.
So,
alone in the dark,
in agony,
I cry out to You,
"Please give me the strength
to walk with You today.
Please show me all
that You would have me do,
until the blessed day
You call me home.
When my family is whole again,
because
we are all together with You."

—C. K. Zimmermann,
December 31, 2017

A Cord of Three Strands

"You turned my wailing into dancing; you removed my sackcloth and clothed me with joy" (Ps 30:11).

Based on statistics alone, our marriage should not have survived after Patrick went to be with Jesus. Our marriage was not strong before the tsunami of NPC hit. Suzanne Cast, our first hospice social worker, shared that she had wondered who would hit the door first, after Patrick died. Statistics told us that marriages of children with disabilities did not survive. We had seen dear friends' marriages strain or break up under the weight of caring for a special-needs child. We also knew that marriages often ended after the death of a child.

The only reason Pastor Gary said he had hope for our relationship was that we both shared a love of Jesus. We knew our marriage was in trouble, and we asked for help before Patrick died. Our church elders visited our home and prayed for us. On that day, Pastor Gary prayed that we would grow closer than we had ever been. His prayer was answered, but it took *a lot* of work. Many, many times Pastor Gary helped us work through issues. He taught us that our first step was to work on our individual relationships with Jesus. He then helped us identify our love languages.

Next, he encouraged us to find ways to serve together. Each of us had experienced the pain of a failed marriage. We learned to go to our knees and call on the Lord during an argument. "A cord of three strands" became our motto. "Though one may be overpowered, two can defend themselves. A cord of three strands is not quickly broken," (Eccl 4:12). We learned we could not forgive past or present hurts on our own. Only though the help of the Lord were we able to forgive one another, let go of the past, and move on. God was doing work in Steve. I loved who he was becoming. God was also refining me, helping me love like Him and forgive like Him.

Pastor Gary said we should forgive quickly and often. Praying together each day, before we arose and again before we fell asleep, helped solidify our relationship. We prayed for others and said the Lord's Prayer together. Being in the Word daily helped us grow closer to the Lord. Attending worship regularly kept us connected to our church family. Serving together in the church nursery and as deacons brought us closer together.

Pastor Gary suggested we renew our wedding vows. We had not been married in the church, and our relationship needed to go from a contract to a covenant. So, on the twenty-five-year anniversary of our first date, Pastor Gary officiated as we renewed our wedding vows at the foot of the crosses on the hill overlooking PEPC. Bob and Meg Paige, the chaplains who had served us in hospice when Patrick died, stood up as our best man and maid of honor. They had taught us a lot about how to make a marriage work. Our home fellowship group served as witnesses. We chose the music "Love Is Not a Fight" from the movie, *Fireproof.* The song described angels guarding the door of a relationship. Our home fellowship group were the angels in our lives, promising to do an intervention if we split up. They knew we loved to dance, and they gave us dance lessons as a vow renewal gift. During our ceremony, Pastor Gary encouraged us to make time to enjoy one another. Dancing together helped us learn how to work and play together.

Okay, Lord, Use Me

> God, I'm not trying to rule the roost, I don't want to be king of the mountain. I haven't meddled where I have no business or fantasized grandiose plans. I've kept my feet on the ground, I've cultivated a quiet heart. Like a baby content in its mother's arms, my soul is a baby content. (Ps 131: 1–2 MSG)

Watching Patrick die broke me. I believe God used that horrific experience to bring me to the end of myself. I had to give up thinking I was strong and could do life on my own. I had to give Him all my hopes and dreams for a "normal" family life and grandchildren. I had to learn to accept that those ideas were not what He had planned for me. Patrick was a gift from God. Losing Patrick, when he was sixteen, *was not at all* what I wanted to happen in my life.

Then I realized that it was not *my* life—it was a gift *from Him,* to be used *by Him* to bring glory *to Him. I had no choice but to trust Him.* I was still on Earth, so He must have a purpose for my being here. The only thing that made sense was to serve Him until He called me home. When I handed everything over to Him and said, "Okay, Lord, use me," then

I experienced peace. I was finally content in His loving embrace. Do waves of grief still crash over me? Yes. Does the evil one still whisper cruel lies to me in the darkness? Yes, oh yes. *But I am never alone.* Jesus is there to tenderly sustain me until He calls me home.

Chapter Twelve

Cindy's Reflections

When I returned home from Haiti, I was not the same woman who had stepped on the plane seven days earlier. Shortly after our trip, I shared what I had learned with the PEPC congregation during Sunday services. "The months after Patrick died were a dark time for us," I said. "I didn't understand why I was still here when I just wanted to be with Patrick in heaven. Then God asked me to do something. He called. I answered, and I'm glad I did, because I believe God sent me on that trip, so I would learn, without a doubt, that I was part of God's global family in Christ. Now I truly understand that the plans God has for me are far better than anything I could ever imagine." I believe He kept me safe and healthy during the trip to Haiti so that I could focus on the lessons He wanted me to learn.

My husband, Steve, and I felt the Lord calling us to join PEPC's team serving on a Petros Network medical mission trip to Africa, in October of that same year. We were blessed to serve as prayer warriors at the TESFA Center's free clinic in Gojo, Ethiopia.[7]

Our relationships with God and one another deepened immeasurably as we saw God on the move in that country. We experienced powerful worship at a local church led by Pastor Abebe in Gojo. Together we prayed with him over patients in English and Amharic. We saw him cast out demons. God chose that clinic in a remote village of Africa to reveal to us the power of prayer. We prayed intensely as a team and witnessed what I would compare to a biblical miracle (Mk 2: 1-12). A sick man, severely dehydrated and with a pulse so weak the doctor could not feel it, was carried into the clinic on a woven couch. With medicine, IV fluids, and hours of our fervent prayer, he was able to walk out of the clinic, unaided. He called. We answered. Because we trusted Him, we were able to see God work through us in Ethiopia.

Just a few short months later, back home in Colorado, as I prepared to return to Haiti for a second trip, as an adult leader with the PEPC youth group, I was hoping to spend time with the young boy to whom I had given Patrick's wheelchair the year before. I wanted to share with his parents how God had helped Steve and me through our hardest days and darkest nights. I was asked to share how my faith had grown during a PEPC mission trip fundraiser.

These are the notes of what the Lord urged me to say.

"Thank you for being here tonight to support PEPC's student mission trip to Haiti. My name is Cindy Zimmermann. Most of you know me as Patrick's mom. God willing, this will be my second trip to the Fond Blanc Orphanage.[8] I was blessed to be a leader on last year's trip. Thank you to all of you who supported my trip financially and through prayer in 2017. God used that experience *powerfully,* to draw me closer in my walk with Him, and I am so excited to see what He wants me to learn on this year's trip.

"Last summer, my heart was hurting from the loss of Patrick, and I did not know why God was calling me to the children at the orphanage. I came to understand that He wanted me to see that I am part of God's global family in Christ and to *trust Him in all things.* Since returning from that mission trip, I am learning to experience life with Christ as a *daily adventure in trust.* I am in the Word and praying constantly. This has helped me cope with my grief and find renewed purpose in life.

"You've probably heard or sung Hillsong United's song, 'Hosanna.' It asks God to break our hearts for the things that break His as we dedicate our lives to His kingdom's cause. Going to Haiti helped me see what *truly* breaks the heart of Christ. Although Haiti has captured my heart, it *is* an assault on the senses. From the air, Haiti, surrounded by turquoise waters, looks like a verdant green island, with veins of tan running through it. As the plane descends, the assault begins. Endless lines of shanties with corrugated rooves appear next to the runway. Noise, heat, humidity, and smoke from burning garbage attack you when you step out of the airport. A sea of beautiful dark faces stare at you. Last year, I could sense when the harsh reality of Haiti's daily life struck the students. Driving though crazy traffic, their happy voices were silenced when they saw a dead woman, in the middle of the road, her tiny bare feet peeking out from under a bloody tarp. Raucous traffic swerved around her.

We think she had been riding on a moto (motorcycle) when she was killed.

"On our trip, we will travel briefly through Port au Prince before heading to the country. Roads will be lined with trash. Smoke and dust will fill our nostrils. The difference between our sheltered American lives and life in Haiti will quickly become apparent. Haitians, both people and their animals, are sinewy, strong, and resilient because of the daily challenges they face. As we drive to the orphanage and the road changes from pavement to rough, rocky road, we will begin to see splashes of vibrant reddish orange color—the Flamboyant tree.

"With your support, we are able to be the hands and feet of Christ in a country ravaged by poverty. I understand American poverty—I grew up *in* it and escaped *from* it. For over twenty years, I have taught in low-income schools. Now I serve children in an impoverished neighborhood of Denver. Haiti's poverty, though, is *overwhelming* in its desperation. PEPC students will see and experience how the light of Christ can bring change in such a place.

"Just like the Flamboyant tree splashes the Haitian landscape with color, on this trip, PEPC students will see where the hand of Christ has been, touching lives. They will see it in the colorful school uniforms of children walking to and from Christian schools, along the dusty roads. They will see it in how the children at the orphanage are filled with light and love, because they have experienced the love of Christ through *them.* Thank you, again, for your support of PEPC's mission trip to Haiti.

"Steve and I will continue to listen to and work hard for the Lord, but I won't kid you. *Some days just hurt because Patrick is not here with us.* Believing he is with God helps us put one foot in front of the other. God has shown us that *He is faithful in all things.*

"Sometimes God sends hugs and kisses, like a gentle nicker from a rescue horse, a caring smile from a friend, or a hug from a little boy named Steve in Haiti. God also shows His love by sending people like Pastor Gary to walk alongside us in the deepest valleys of our grief. I will have *lots* of questions to ask God, when He finally calls me home. After I fall down in worship, I'll ask him to please show me all the ways Patrick's short life and unwavering faith in Jesus impacted the lives of others, like ripples in a pond."

Chapter Thirteen

Pastor Gary's Reflections

Walking Alongside a Family in Crisis

I asked Pastor Gary to share what he was thinking as he prepared to meet with us for the first time. He is trained in biblical counseling and has walked alongside many people who are hurting and desperately need to feel the Lord's presence. Pastor Gary is a humble man with amazing gifts from God. He has been given the ability to connect with people, and Christ's love flows through him. Our hope is that his wisdom, gained from years of serving the Lord, will help other pastors preparing to step into a situation where they will be ministering to a family in crisis.

Here is what Pastor Gary had to say about that first meeting:

> "When I was driving over to Fika, I was thinking, 'Lord, you have created this opportunity. Let me represent you well.

Help me to hear what I need to hear.' One of my life verses is 'Rejoice always, pray continually, give thanks in all circumstances; for this is God's will for you in Christ Jesus' (1 Thes5:16–18).

"Our church secretary, Vicki, had given me your names and told me about your request to learn more about heaven. I'm praying all the time. I was praying, 'Okay, Lord. Let me to get to know this mom and this son. How can I serve them? This is about you, not about me. I want to be your ambassador.' I was thinking about Ephesians 6:19. 'Pray also for me, that whenever I speak, words may be given me so that I will fearlessly make known the mystery of the gospel.'

"I wasn't afraid. Before Christ, as a young man, I was really almost paralyzed by what people would think of me. Therefore, I wouldn't speak. Satan wants us to be afraid. The scriptures are full of places where Jesus says, 'Fear not.' I'm not afraid of much. Part of it comes with age, and part of it comes because God has revealed himself to me so many times, saying, 'I will never leave you nor forsake you' (Heb 13:5 ESV). I never feel alone in any situation.

"I've had many years of life experience in testimony of how God has worked in situations that could have been stressful. God has taught me to trust Him to give me the words, whether it was in a job interview, an intense counseling situation, or interacting with generals while working for Youth for Christ on a military base in Germany.

"So, I'm at a place in life where I've learned to trust that the Holy Spirit will create a space, fill that, and give me the right words to say. I didn't have an agenda that afternoon. If you have a set agenda, that can appear to be disingenuous. I was thinking, how can I serve this family? I just wanted to see if I could be an encouragement to you guys.

"I don't have a formula. Every counseling situation is different. I want to lead people to the place where they encounter Jesus. I don't want to get in the way of that. My simple philosophy in ministry is relationships, relationships, relationships. How do you speak truth and love to somebody? Wait for God to reveal how to speak truth and love. One of the skills or gifts God has given me is to be a good listener.

"As a pastor, I get people to talk about themselves. I just listen. I ask questions that show that I really care and that I want to be available. If He prompts me to ask about their faith or lack of faith in Jesus, I will. I pray that I can listen well and then speak accordingly. I don't want to mess it up. I'm asking God to help me, so that I don't just talk. I make sure that I'm saying something meaningful. Over the years, God has also given me peace that silence is okay. In my younger years, I would have needed to fill the space.

"For me, the ministry of presence comes from Col 1:27 (ESV): 'To them God chose to make known how great among the Gentiles are the riches of the glory of this mystery, which is Christ in you, the hope of glory.' In pastoral care, embody the Holy Spirit in the particular space to which God has sent you."

Here are some specific pieces of advice for walking with a family in crisis.

- Expect God to show up.
- Expect that He is going to give you the right thing to say and the right time to say it.
- Know your limitations—know how to direct people to the right place.
- Have access to other professionals who are better equipped than you are to handle difficult situations.
- Don't try to be the hero.

To reiterate—be slow to speak and quick to listen. Just as a Stephen minister is trained to be a listener, the whole thing is to listen. Listen and respond accordingly.

A Sacred Season

"Patrick's faith was alive after our meeting at Fika, when he prayed to believe in Jesus and trusted him with his life. It was obvious when he got baptized, and then after that marker in his faith, how he wanted more and more of Jesus. That was the beginning of a sacred season in Patrick's life as his earth-suit declined, and he prepared to join his heavenly Father. Cindy pleaded with Steve not to try to sabotage Patrick's faith. Steve did not share his own doubts about the existence of God with Patrick. Cindy and Steve were so significant in the development of Patrick's young faith. Together they led him in reading and memorizing scriptures, prayed as a family, played and sang Christian songs, and brought him to church each week. He wanted to sit right down in the front pew, so he could feel closer to God.

"Patrick's smile and joy for life was contagious, not to mention his love for people. His faith became so tangible that it was encouraging and empowering to me and many others, especially how God used him to soften his dad's heart to eventually surrender to the same Jesus that Patrick passionately loved. I shared the story of his life-giving faith with those in our community, much like how we have people share their kingdom stories at church. His story speaks to people's hearts, so that they might consider fully surrendering and trusting in Jesus. Patrick, at fifteen years old and knowing his time on Earth was short, never stopped enthusiastically sharing Jesus with others.

"Patrick is one of my heroes because of his amazing faith in Jesus in the most adverse of circumstances. He was such an encouragement to others in our church family and beyond. God used Patrick's life and testimony to impact the lives of many at PEPC and in our community. He continues to do so through the testimony of his mother and father and their faithfulness to Jesus and the PEPC family."

Boys, Baseball, and Trusting God's Plan for our Lives

Pastor Gary and Patrick shared a love of baseball. They would discuss the sport during Pastor Gary's visits to the Faded Rose Ranch. They also loved the Denver Broncos, Culver's Cement Mixers, and Wendy's cheeseburgers. I truly believe that our initial meeting with Pastor McCusker at Fika Coffee House was one of God's divine appointments. God knew that Patrick needed to hear about Christ from a man's man with a missionary's heart, someone he could look up to. If anyone else had walked through the door that day at Fika, I don't know if Patrick would have accepted Christ. But God knew who needed to deliver His message of good news. I'm so glad Pastor Gary stepped up to bat as the home run hitter for God's team that day at Fika.

Pastor Gary coached high school baseball for many years. He and his wife, Debi, also lead a coed slow pitch softball team for PEPC. I asked him to share if he ever questioned the path God had chosen for him—a path that didn't include playing baseball in college or professionally. His answer surprised me because my faith is not as strong as his and I often have "discussions" with God when I am second-guessing His plan for my life. I also asked him to share how his faith and his coaching philosophy intersect.

"Faith is one of my key spiritual gifts. I don't have a lot of doubts or questions. I didn't question God. I may not be able to articulate all the answers correctly in a theological debate, but in my heart, I know that God is God, and His truth is truth. I wasn't a star, so I didn't have grandiose ideas about a future in baseball. My players will sometimes ask me which position I played. I explain that I was cut from the team as a sophomore. I never heard why, but I think it was because I missed a practice when I chose to go to a basketball tournament to watch a friend play. I wasn't thinking, and I didn't tell the coach I was going. When I came back from the tournament, I was nixed. I was devastated. I loved baseball, though, and stayed connected to the sport by umpiring games for younger players.

"Now, as a coach, it's a tender time for me if I must cut a player. I am very careful to explain why they are being cut. I tell them, 'Don't let this define you. Let's find another place where you can succeed.'

"The friend in the basketball tournament, Gary Parsons, would help lead me to Christ by taking me to Young Life (YL) activities. At YL, I was introduced to a Jesus who was different than my Catholic upbringing had taught me. I learned about having a relationship with Christ. Later, I went to a weekend camp at Mount Hermon in California. Some guy was sharing a testimony that resonated with me. That's my story. That began my pilgrimage toward Christ. In 1971, at a YL summer camp in Canada, I stood up and said I wanted to commit my life to Christ.

"I trained to be a physical education teacher and coach, because I wanted to influence young people. I thought I could represent Christ that way. I later became a Youth for Christ missionary, a youth pastor, and now serve as a family life pastor. With coaching and playing for PEPC, God has really given baseball back to me in different ways to still have that fulfillment.

"If I'm in the dugout, I know God is there. Christ is in us. We bring the presence of Christ into any situation. You can't talk about God in schools, but I've never been rejected from a public school. You can be in schools. If I'm there, I'm not really saying much; I'm just sitting around, just being there. I get to become a vessel that God can use.

"That's why the ministry of presence is so important. The tabernacle was brought to the people of Israel. Now that we have that presence within us, through the Holy Spirit, we become a tabernacle. We become a place where God dwells. My pocket Bible is my dagger. It's the New Testament, Psalms, and Proverbs. The sword I carry is the whole Bible. When I go from here to the practice field, I'm His ambassador. I get to hit the balls to the players, but I'm looking for the opportunity to help them *get it.*

"I was recently invited to speak at a Colorado Dugout Club prayer breakfast. The Colorado Dugout Club is an annual high school coaching clinic. The topic was, 'Why Do We Coach?' A game is just a game. As a Christian, it must be more than that.

My Coaching Philosophy is the Four Cs.

- Character—Develop their character.
- Competence—Help them develop their competence when hitting, fielding, running, and catching.
- Chemistry—How do you become a good team player for one another, not just for yourself?
- Commitment—Be committed to your team, your school, your family, and your sport.

For a season of your life, make the most of it.

"I look at everything I do with that in mind. Better character, better player. Better teammate, better person. I need to model that. I can talk about it all day long, but if I don't model it, then it doesn't have much credibility."

How did I Serve the Zimmermanns?

"Steve, Cindy, and I brainstormed the following list of the ways that I served them.

- Meeting with Cindy and Patrick at Fika the first time
- Baptizing Patrick at PEPC
- Praying regularly
- Having church family and staff pray for them
- Anointing them
- Talking with them each week before or after church
- Encouraging them to grow closer to the Lord
- Assigning people to watch over them and report back to me
- Eating lunches with Patrick
- Giving them several books about heaven, books about marriage, a book about youth ministry
- Visiting their home frequently
- Giving a special Bible to Patrick with my life verses listed inside the front cover and high-lighted within each book
- Going to Children's Hospital for diagnosis, praying at the beginning and ending of the appointment
- Finding many people to help repair the Faded Rose Ranch
- Assigning Stephen Ministers to Steve and Cindy, even though they were resistant and needed lots of encouragement to accept help
- Youth Action Bible provided by our youth pastor
- Encouraging them to read *The Message* together
- Encouraging Cindy to purchase a study Bible

- Connecting them to a home fellowship
- Having elders visit their home and pray with the family
- Baptizing Steve and Cindy at Aurora Reservoir
- Calling and visiting during Patrick's hospice stay
- Assigning chaplains Bob and Meg Paige to be available the night Patrick died when I was out of town
- Planning the funeral
- Officiating the funeral and the graveside service
- Grief counseling
- Connecting Cindy with grief counselors outside of PEPC
- Helping them sell their handicapped van to another PEPC family
- Analyzing and discussing Prepare/Enrich Marriage Inventory results twice, administered a year apart
- Counseling despite daunting numbers on the Prepare/Enrich Marriage Inventory
- Having PEPC sponsor them for Weekend to Remember, a marriage enrichment retreat[9]
- Officiating their vow renewal ceremony on the hill at PEPC
- Encouraging them to serve as deacons (That has helped them stay connected to PEPC when the evil one told them to leave.)
- Encouraging them to attend training to become youth mentors
- Mailing a grief booklet to them each quarter, the year after Patrick died
- Encouraging them to attend GriefShare sessions

- Inviting Steve to join Men in the Arena men's weekly Bible study
- Connecting them with a Christian financial counselor
- Counseling them during job searches
- Helping them write this book about Patrick's faith as part of the grief process"

What Did I Learn? What Would I Do Differently?

"I was invited into the Zimmermann's life, so I knew that I had a responsibility to reach them with the love of Christ and to lure them to Jesus, especially when I found out Steve was hostile to God and that Cindy needed to make a head-to-heart connection. They needed comforting and encouragement to know they were not alone. I leaned into that. I am a hugger, and I believe the ministry of appropriate touch is critical. I'm always going to be a touch person. When I learned that Cindy had suffered abuse in her past and was extremely uncomfortable with physical touch, including side-hugs and holding hands during prayer, I adjusted my response. It was a little bit of a shock. I was sad. If I had known sooner, I would have changed how I was interacting with them immediately. They had let me into a sacred space, and I didn't want to do anything to hurt them or to damage that relationship.

"Steve and Cindy needed clearly delineated boundaries to feel safe when they worked with me because they had experienced so much hurt and betrayal in other relationships. As we worked on this book, we were careful to protect our pastoral relationship. Steve, Cindy, and I met together to discuss edits and revisions to this book. Our communications about the manuscript always included all three of us. We did those things deliberately to safeguard our working alliance.

"Here are some general guidelines I use in pastoral counseling. As a rule, I do not meet with a woman alone for ongoing counseling. If I need to have an initial meeting to determine a woman's counseling needs, I keep my office door open and have a church staff member close by. I invite that staff member into the office if we are going to pray. I then refer that woman to a female Christian counselor. I give side-hugs, not full hugs to women. These guidelines help create a safe space in counseling situations.

"I serve on the board of directors for an organization called Men in the Arena. It was originally called The Great Hunt for God. One of our publications, *The Playbook*, written by Jim Ramos, lists specific guardrails that men (and women) can use to protect their marriages.[10] These guardrails can also apply to pastors when counseling couples or individuals. Men in the Arena has given me permission to share these guardrails in hopes that they will help pastors serving families in crisis.

Guardrail 1

> Never develop an emotional connection to another woman. (Prv 29:3; 5:3).

Guardrail 2

Never be alone with a woman behind closed doors, in public, at 'meetings,' in vehicles, and so forth. (Prv 8:11–12; Lk 12:2–3).

Guardrail 3

Never engage in any negative talk with a woman about your marriage, wife, or sex life. (Prv 18:22; 24:3; 30:20; 1 Pt 3:7; Heb 13:4).

Guardrail 4

Never compliment a woman in a way that would elicit an emotional response, unless your wife is somehow woven into the compliment. (Prv 17:24; Mal 2:14). Example: 'I noticed you colored your hair. My wife colors her hair too, but I love her no matter what color it is.'

Guardrail 5

Never have a counseling relationship with another woman (one and done). (Prv 2:16; 14:8).

Guardrail 6

Never make physical contact with a sensual area of another woman. (Prv 5:20; 6:26). Example: Give a side-hug as opposed to a full-frontal hug.

Guardrail 7

Never make foul, rude, or sexual comments to a woman. (Prv 10:23, 31; 7:5; Eph 5:4, 12; Col 3:8).

Guardrail 8

Never give a gift or card to another woman that is only from you. (Prv 9:12). Example: Sign the gift or card from you and your wife and use words like 'we' and 'us.'

Guardrail 9

Never have non-business-related communication with another woman (text, private message, Facebook, phone calls, etc.) (Prv 1:20 and 2:6).

Guardrail 10

Never assume your wife is living by your standards. Be engaged. (Prv 2:12; 4:5; 5:1)."

Chapter Fourteen

Home Runs for Heaven

Over four hundred people attended Patrick's Memorial Service. At least twelve people raised their hands to say they wanted to accept Jesus Christ as their Lord and Savior that day. Steve and I pray for them often, asking God to help their faith develop *deep roots.* During the service, many people shared how Patrick's life and faith impacted their lives. Tom Woods, Patrick's youth baseball coach, described how he would pray that Patrick would connect with the ball when he was at bat. I was also praying on the sidelines during Patrick's games. I remember talking to God and saying, *I know it's is such a small thing, but could You please let Patrick get a piece of the ball, please, Lord?* This was years before Patrick's NPC diagnosis, and when the disease was just beginning to affect his coordination and spatial awareness. We had no idea why it was getting harder and harder for Patrick to hit the ball. He was a trooper and did his best, even when it became difficult to make contact.

We couldn't know that *God had a much bigger plan* for Patrick than making contact in a youth baseball game. I understand now that Patrick's life was to be a shining example of how hope in Christ can bring us through life's hardest challenges. If sharing his story can bring people to Christ, then Patrick is truly hitting home runs for heaven!

Endnotes

1   GriefShare. I heard the tapestry metaphor explained in GriefShare Week 6. Learn more at https://www.griefshare.org/.

2   Stephen Ministry. Pastor Gary urged us to accept the help of Stephen ministers from our church. We're so glad he did. For more information, search https://www.stephenministries.org/stephenministry/default.cfm/917?mnb=1.

3   Nicky Gumbel, *Bible in One Year*, 'Day 304: The Surprising Secret of Freedom', Copyright © by Nicky Gumbel 2018.

4   John Gillespie Magee, Jr., "High Flight," poem written by in 1941.

5   Lisa J. Barila, "I See You, Patrick" Copyright © 2016. We are so thankful that Lisa Barila shared her poem about Patrick at his memorial service and in this book.

6   GriefShare. Steve and I found GriefShare classes to be very helpful in learning to process our grief. https://www.griefshare.org/.

7   Petros Network organized the medical mission trip to Gojo, Ethiopia. You can learn more at https://petrosnetwork.org/.

8   Fond Blanc Foundation runs the orphanage where PEPC students and Cindy served. Find out more at https://fondblanc.org/.

9   Weekend to Remember. https://www.familylife.com/weekend-to-remember/. PEPC sponsored us so that we could attend a Weekend to Remember. It was helpful to us on our journey of reconciliation.

10 Jim Ramos, The Great Hunt for God, The Playbook, Volume 1 Copyright © 2012, 144–146. Great Hunt for God recently changed its name to Men in the Arena. We are thankful that this organization allowed us to share the invaluable guardrails in this book. Learn more at https://www.thegreathuntforgod.com/.